Let Me Rephrase That!

Your Layman's Guide to Abrogations

Includes topical excerpts from the following Boreal Books on Islam, the Prophet and the Koran:

Shared Prophets

Getting to Know Allah

Women and the Koran

The Islamic Hereafter

Allah's War Against the Unbelievers

From Merchant to Messenger

Alice Visits a Mosque to Learn About Judgement Day

1,001 Sayings and Deeds of the Prophet Muhammad

Between a Pillar and a Hard Place

Bernard Payeur

Cover art is a rendition of a picture of George Burns from a poster for the 1977 Warner Bros. film "Oh, God!"

ISBN 978-1-928023-07-4

Boreal Books
www.boreal.ca

A la mémoire de:

Stéphane Charbonnier

Franck Brinsolaro

Ahmed Merabet

Jean Cabut

Georges Wolinski

Bernard Verlhac

Frédéric Boisseau

Elsa Cayat

Philippe Honoré

Bernard Maris

Mustapha Ourrad

Michel Renaud

Contents

Introduction

Of all the incongruities that devotees of a religion steeped in incongruities have to accept, the concept of abrogation has to be the most outlandish. Abrogation, i.e. retraction, annulment, cancellation ... is common in the real world as better information replaces old information. In the world of revealed truths, immutable facts revealed to a mortal by a god, abrogation should not even be the exception. It defies logic, and there lies the incongruity, the weirdness.

For the rational mind, it is inconceivable that a god, in a book He claims to have written, in Arabic no less (classical Arabic* is assumed), at the beginning of time, if not earlier, and in which He lays claim to infallibility, has to retract, annul, abolish, modify ... what He said earlier.

The incongruity takes even more bizarre proportions when you consider that God carved His book in a tablet which He keeps close, and from which He quotes to the angel Gabriel who will then communicate to the Prophet Muhammad the latest unassailable fact from on High about the observable universe and our place in it – an incontrovertible observation which God himself will later prove, by second-guessing Himself, to have been no such thing.

> 85:21 Yet, it is a glorious Qur'an,
>
> 85:22 In a Well-Preserved Tablet.
>
> ----
>
> 43:3 We have made it an Arabic Qur'an that perchance you may understand.
>
> 43:4 And, indeed, it is in the Mother of the Book, with Us, lofty and wise.

A saying of the Prophet places the Koran on the Throne itself, in all likelihood on Allah's lap.

> **Narrated Abu Huraira:**
>
> Allah's Apostle said, "When Allah completed the creation, He wrote in His Book which is with Him on His Throne, 'My Mercy overpowers My Anger.'"
>
> *Bukhari 54.416*

Even with this handy allegedly flawless aide-memoire at His disposal, which an omniscient god should have no need, God still stumbles. It is absurd!

Contemporary scholars, unlike their mostly Arab classical counterparts who came up with the more than two hundred abrogated revelations around the eleventh century, are divided on the concept of abrogation, and the uncomfortable contradictions it entails. The Arabs were, and most still are eminently at ease with opposites:

> This people was black and white not merely in clarity, but in apposition. Their thoughts were at ease only in extremes ... they never compromised; they pursued the logic of several incompatible opinions to absurd ends, without perceiving the incongruity.

> *T.E. Lawrence, Seven Pillars of Wisdom*

The modern potential believer is not as easily accommodating of concepts that defy common sense, as were the converts of old or those fortunate enough to have been born to believing parents and therefore benefiting from a rigorous uncompromising indoctrination into reveal truths from early childhood.

There is a very common ceremony practiced throughout most of the Muslim world called Khatmi-Qur'an. It is the ceremony to recognize and celebrate a child's first full reading of the Koranic text in Arabic. Muslim children in traditional Islamic societies or families are expected to have read and more or less understood the Koran, in Arabic, from cover to cover before they reach the age of seven.

The difficulty in getting converts to accept the inherent absurdity of a know-it-all omnipotent god not getting it right the first, even the second time around may explain the attempt by contemporary scholars to refute the very concept of abrogation as did Muhammad Asad (1900-92) who argued that classical scholars misinterpreted passages relating to abrogation, citing verse 10:64 as evidence of the immutability of Allah's Words.

> 10:64 Theirs is the good news in the present life and the Hereafter. And there will be no alteration of the Words of Allah. That is the great triumph.

Not so according to another contemporary expert Ahmad von Denffer (1949-present). For this eminent scholar, understanding abrogation is central to the correct application of Allah's laws. Denffer quotes four revelations to Asad's one, where Allah admits to changing His mind.

> 2:106 Whichever verse We abrogate or cause to be forgotten, We bring instead a better or similar one. Do you not know that Allah has the power over all things?

13:39 Allah blots out and confirms what He pleases; and with Him is the Mother of the Book.

16:101 And if We replace a verse by another – and Allah knows best what He reveals – they say: "You [Muhammad] are only a forger." Surely, most of them do not know.

17:86 If We please, We certainly can blot out that which We have revealed to you (O Muhammad); then you would find no guardian to assist you against Us.

Allah even acknowledged that His changing His mind was causing problems for His Messenger whose detractors thought it strange, an omnipotent all-knowing god who could not get it right the first time. These open-minded individual reached the only possible conclusion: their kin, the first would-be Arab spokesperson for the Almighty was making it up as he went along, and told him so to his face, calling him a forger in revelation 16:101. The Arabs of old knew more than Allah was willing to admit judging by the non-answer Gabriel communicated to the Prophet Muhammad in response to the forgery accusation.

16:102 Say: "The Holy Spirit has brought it down from our Lord in truth, in order to reassure the believers, as a guidance and good news to those who submit.

----

* **Classical Arabic (CA)**, also known as Qur'anic or Koranic Arabic, is the form of the Arabic language used in literary text from Umayyad and Abbasid times (7th to 9th centuries). It is based on the Medieval dialects of Arab tribes. Modern Standard Arabic (MSA) is the direct descendent [of Classical Arabic]... While the lexis and stylistics of Modern Standard Arabic are different from Classical Arabic, the morphology and syntax have remain basically unchanged (thought MSA uses a subset of the syntactic structure available in CA). The vernacular dialects, however, have changed more dramatically...

Tradition has it that the caliph Ali, after reading the Qur'an with errors in it, asked Abu al-Aswad al Du'ali to write a work codifying Arabic grammar. Khalil ibn Ahmad would later write Kitab al-Ayn, the first dictionary of Arabic ..."

From Modern Arabic poetry 1800-1970: the development of its *forms* and themes by Shmuel Moreh

A Harvest of Contradictions

The first *official* Koran was compiled after the Prophet's death by a scribe by the name of Thabit. He was urged to do so by the successor of the Prophet as leader of the believer, after the death of many of the best memorisers of the Koran at the battle of Yamaha during the so-called War of the Apostates, a rebellion against Muslim rule following the death of God's Messenger.

Narrated Zaid bin Thabit Al-Ansari who was one of those who used to write the Divine Revelation:

Abu Bakr sent for me after the (heavy) casualties among the warriors (of the battle) of Yamama (where a great number of Qurra' (reciters of the Koran) were killed). Umar was present with Abu Bakr who said, "Umar has come to me and said, 'The people have suffered heavy casualties on the day of (the battle of) Yamama, and I am afraid that there will be more casualties among the Qurra' (those who know the Qur'an by heart) at other battle-fields, whereby a large part of the Qur'an may be lost, unless you collect it. And I am of the opinion that you should collect the Qur'an.'"

Abu Bakr added, "I said to Umar, 'How can I do something which Allah's Apostle has not done?'"

Umar said (to me), "By Allah, it is (really) a good thing." So Umar kept on pressing, trying to persuade me to accept his proposal, till Allah opened my bosom for it and I had the same opinion as Umar.

(Zaid bin Thabit added:) Umar was sitting with him, Abu Bakr, and was not speaking to me).

"You are a wise young man and we do not suspect you (of telling lies or of forgetfulness): and you used to write the Divine Inspiration for Allah's Apostle. Therefore, look for the Qur'an and collect it (in one manuscript)."

By Allah, if he (Abu Bakr) had ordered me to shift one of the mountains (from its place) it would not have been harder for me than what he had ordered me concerning the collection of the Qur'an. I said to both of them, "How dare you do a thing which the Prophet has not done?"

Abu Bakr said, "By Allah, it is (really) a good thing." So I kept on arguing with him about it till Allah opened my bosom for that which He had opened the bosoms of Abu

Bakr and Umar. So I started locating Quranic material and collecting it from parchments, scapula, leaf-stalks of date palms and from the memories of men (who knew it by heart).

I found with Khuzaima two Verses of Surat-at-Tauba which I had not found with anybody else, (and they were): "Verily there has come to you an Apostle (Muhammad) from amongst yourselves. It grieves him that you should receive any injury or difficulty He (Muhammad) is ardently anxious over you (to be rightly guided)" (9:128)

The manuscript on which the Quran was collected, remained with Abu Bakr till Allah took him unto Him, and then with Umar till Allah took him unto Him, and finally it remained with Hafsa, Umar's daughter.

Bukhari 60.201

The contradictions in the Koran were evident early on. Umar asked Thabit about these. He replied that it was not up to him to change the hearsay evidence he had collected about what the Prophet preached Allah had revealed to him via the angel Gabriel.

The final official version of the Koran was rushed into production during the Caliphate of Uthman, the third caliph, for reasons explained in the following hadith:

Narrated Anas bin Malik:

Hudhaifa bin Al-Yaman came to Uthman at the time when the people of Sham and the people of Iraq were Waging war to conquer Arminya and Adharbijan. Hudhaifa was afraid of their (the people of Sham and Iraq) differences in the recitation of the Qur'an, so he said to Uthman, "O chief of the Believers! Save this nation before they differ about the Book (Quran) as Jews and the Christians did before."

So Uthman sent a message to Hafsa saying, "Send us the manuscripts of the Qur'an so that we may compile the Qur'anic materials in perfect copies and return the manuscripts to you."

Hafsa sent it to Uthman. Uthman then ordered Zaid bin Thabit, Abdullah bin AzZubair, Said bin Al-As and Abdur Rahman bin Harith bin Hisham to rewrite the manuscripts in perfect copies.

Uthman said to the three Quraishi men, "In case you disagree with Zaid bin Thabit on any point in the Qur'an, then write it in the dialect of Quraish, the Qur'an was revealed in their tongue."

They did so, and when they had written many copies, Uthman returned the original manuscripts to Hafsa.

Uthman sent to every Muslim province one copy of what they had copied, and ordered that all the other Qur'anic materials, whether written in fragmentary manuscripts or whole copies, be burnt.

Said bin Thabit added, "A Verse from Surat Ahzab was missed by me when we copied the Qur'an and I used to hear Allah's Apostle reciting it. So we searched for it and found it with Khuzaima bin Thabit Al-Ansari. (That Verse was): 'Among the Believers are men who have been true in their covenant with Allah.'" (33:23)

Bukhari 61.510

It was left to future generation of scholars, most of them from the eight to eleventh century to review the document which the eminent English historian Thomas Carlyle [1795 - 1881] described as "a confused, jumble, crude, incondite, endless iteration..." and come up with a list of revelations, which is still being argued over fourteen centuries later as to which revealed truths were totally or partially abrogated by something Allah publicized subsequently.

The Koran is very much a hodgepodge of paragraphs or verses called ayats most of which bear little resemblance in whatever translation you consult to what we understand as a verse i.e. "writing arranged with a metrical rhythm, typically having a rhyme".

The Bible, the King James Version, is about 791,328 words, more than 10 times the number of words in the Koran. It covers a period of more than a thousand years and contains a cast of thousands. For such a monumental work it is surprisingly well ordered.

The Koran, on the other hand, is the inspiration of just one man, from revelations ostensibly from God communicated over a period of just twenty-three years between 610 and 632 A.D. inclusively.

Unlike the Bible, the Koran is somewhat disorganized. There is no timeline. The only allowance given to any kind of order is the sequencing of most of the 114 surahs i.e. chapters from longest to shortest and a determination made by scholars as to what surahs were received during the Prophet's time in Mecca, before he was run out of town. God's Messenger was forced to flee for his life, in part, for insisting that all would join their forefathers in Hell unless they became Muslims, and for what the leadership of the city saw as a ploy by their kin to rule over them by declaring himself the Almighty's ultimate spokesperson, with the immense power that conveyed.

The fear that Muhammad wanted to rule unopposed would prove a fear well-founded after the Prophet arrived in Medina where he was initially welcomed by the Jews and Arabs of the oasis city who were receptive to a mediator to settle disputes.

> 33:36 It is not up to any believer, man or woman, when Allah and His Messenger have passed a judgement, to have any choice in their affairs. Whoever disobeys Allah and His Messenger have gone astray in a manifest manner.

The Before and After Solution

The revelations received during the Prophet's stay in Medina, which became his home and powerbase until his death, are known as the Medinan surahs: 2, 3, 4, 5, 8, 9, 13, 22, 24, 33, 47, 48, 49, 55, 57, 58, 59, 60, 61, 62, 63, 64, 65, 66, 76, 98, 110.

Scholars are in general agreement that the Medinan chapters supersede Meccan surahs, not only because of the timeframe in which there were received, but also because it was at Medina that Allah communicated his more obdurate instructions such as to kill the pagans and to give Christians and Jews the option of paying the jizya, a poll tax to avoid converting (more about this tax in the chapter Verse of the Tax). In the Medinan surahs it is clear that Allah has undergone a transformation and is no longer the sometimes-tolerant deity whom His Messenger introduced to his Meccan kin.

Some commentator further divide the Medinan period into the Koran sanctioning of total war against the infidels i.e. the polytheist followed by Allah's endorsement of a war against the Jews with the attack on the Jewish settlement of Khaibar (Appendix Khaibar).

I would add a third defining moment, and that would be Allah's sanctioning of attacks on Christians with the Koran's account of the march on the Byzantium settlement of Tabuk (Appendix Tabuk) and the destruction of the Christian mosque of Medina (Appendix Destruction of the Christian Mosque of Medina).

Ascertaining from which period in the Prophet's life a revelation was received is important in determining if something Allah revealed is still valid or has been abrogated i.e. replaced by a subsequent revelation, but it is not, as you will discover, the only criteria.

One Abrogating One

Explanatory Note

Abrogated verses and their abrogator are from WikiIslam, November 12, 2014

WikiIslam uses the words abrogated to identify the verse or parts of a verse that is no longer valid, and abrogator to identify the verse or verses or portion of a verse which has replaced the original. I have adopted their nomenclature.

Where verses are presented side-by-side, the abrogated is on the left, the abrogator on the right. Verses in either column in italics are there for continuity and context only.

Wherever you see the command "say", usually at the beginning of a revelation, this is Allah addressing his spokesperson the Prophet Muhammad, telling him what to say, usually in response to an inquiry or accusation.

Abul A'la Moududi's (also spelt Maududi) [1903-1979] is a pre-eminent Islamic scholar journalist, theologian, Muslim revivalist, Islamist philosopher and the first recipient of the King Faisal International Award for his services to Islam and Islamic studies. Of the more than 120 books he wrote, he is most famous for his magnum opus *The Meaning of the Qur'an*. When Fakhry's crisp translation is not sufficient, it is Moududi I most often turn to for a clarification which I enclose in () if inserted inside a verse.

A one-to-one replacement is the simplest form of abrogation, one verse received earlier is fully or partially replaced by a more current version. The abrogator is often within the same chapter as the verse it is abrogating, an indication that it may have been sent in response to a question from a member of the Prophet's audience during his allocution. Allah confirmed this in a revelation about members of the Prophet's audience sneaking out before His Messenger had finished delivering his latest surah.

> 9:127 And whenever a Surah is revealed, they look at each other [saying]: "Does anyone see you?" Then they turn away. Allah has turned away their hearts, because they are a people who do not understand.

I have no hope of competing with scholars who have spent their lifetime trying to make sense of the idiosyncrasies which saturate

Islamic scriptures including the concept of abrogation about which there is much disagreement as to what is abrogated, with a minority of religious experts questioning the very idea, for it raises doubts, as was mentioned earlier, about the perfection of the Koran, and by extension that of its Author.

Having said that, I do offer, where it exists, contextual and historical information about both the abrogated and the abrogator, and where warranted, state the obvious.

Charity Becomes Compulsory

The fact that the lowest numbered verse abrogated is a revealed truth about charity being desirable but not compulsory to one where the Prophet is empowered to demand it, in and of itself could be considered noteworthy.

2:2 This is the Book which cannot be doubted and is a guidance to the God-fearing.

2:3 Those who believe in the Unseen, perform the prayer and give freely from what We provided for them.

9:103 Take of their wealth voluntary alms to purify and cleanse them therewith; and pray for them, for your prayers are a source of tranquility for them. Allah is All-Hearing, All-Knowing.

The "voluntary alms" whose amount Allah decrees is to be determined and collected by His Messenger have become the obligatory Zakat, the third of the five pillars of Islam.

1. Shahadah, declaring allegiance to God.
2. Salat, daily prayers.
3. Zakat, annual charity.
4. Saum, month-long fasting.
5. Hajj, the pilgrimage to Mecca.

Charity (Zakat) is the only one of the Five Pillars of Islam that has nothing to do with worshipping Allah except perhaps in an indirect sort of way, such as when you give it in furtherance of His Cause.

47:38 There you are; you are called upon to spend freely in Allah's Cause, but some of you are niggardly. Yet he who is niggardly is only niggardly against himself. Allah is the All-Sufficient and you are the destitute. If you turn back, He will replace you by a people other than you, and they will not be like you at all.

Cynics might argue that Allah instinctively appreciated the strategic value of helping people in need in recruiting for His Cause. An understand of the persuasive power of giving that was not lost on the Islamists who, during the catastrophic flooding in Pakistan in 2010 disrupted aid from Western Countries while facilitating the distribution of the inadequate contributions from Islamic regimes; or in Somalia where Allah's militants stopped food shipments from Western nations from reaching famine ravaged portions of the country.

No More Mr. Nice Guy I

Once-upon-time Allah was much more tolerant of other religions.

2:62 The believers (Muslims), the Jews, the Christians and the Sabians – whoever believes in Allah and the Last Day and does what is good, shall receive their reward from their Lord. They shall have nothing to fear and they shall not grieve.

3:85 Whoever seeks a religion other than Islam, it will never be accepted from him, and in the Hereafter he will be one of the losers.

A Change of Direction

As mentioned earlier, if it hadn't been for the Jews of Medina, Islam would have been dead on arrival.

The Jews of Medina began doubting the wisdom of welcoming the Prophet and his followers when, to make ends meet, they started raiding the Meccan caravans which passed between Medina and the Red Sea. These raids would lead to the battle of Badr (Appendix Battle of Badr) which ignited the Arab Civil War and the wars of conquest and annihilation which continue to this day e.g. Islamic State.

After the victory at Badr, God's Messenger felt confident enough to impose his will on his former friends who had become his harshest critics. Two of the three tribes chose exile; one chose to tough it out. A fatal mistake (Appendix Massacre of the Banu Qurayzah)!

Before the Prophet's falling out with the Jews of Medina, the believers prostrated themselves in the direction of Jerusalem during their daily prayers, not Mecca. Before the breakup, Allah did not care in which direction you prayed; He was everywhere after all.

2:115 To Allah belongs the East and the West. So whichever way you turn (while praying), there is Allah's Face. Indeed Allah is Omnipresent and Omniscient.

2:144 Surely, We see your face turned towards heaven (yearning for guidance through revelation). We shall turn you towards a Qibla that will please you. Turn your face then towards the Sacred Mosque (the Sacred Mosque of Mecca, the Ka'ba); and wherever you are turn your faces towards it. Those who were given the Book (the Jews and Christians) certainly know this to be the Truth from their Lord. Allah is not unaware of what they do.

Safa, Marwa and the Religion of Abraham

Islam considers Hagar the legitimate wife of Abraham and her son his first heir and father of the Arabs. In the Koran, Abraham makes near impossible treks across the length of the Arabian Peninsula to pay homage to Allah at Mecca and to visit with Hagar and their son Isma'il (Appendix Abraham at Mecca). Of course, none of these visits are mentioned in the Bible and there is no historical or archaeological evidence of the Patriarch of Muslims and Jews crossing the deserts of Arabia to spend time in Mecca which, at the time, if it existed at all, would have been nothing more than a nomadic settlement.

The entire Hajj ritual is an attempt to recreate the rite Abraham is alleged to have performed to honour Allah when he visited Mecca and His Ka'ba. Over time, Allah was joined at the Ka'ba by other gods, the so-called idols, which caused Him and later His Messenger extreme distress.

During the so-called pagan interlude when Allah had to share his Ka'ba with other gods – and goddesses – the pagans introduced rituals such as going around the Ka'ba naked, probably after having more than a few sips of wine. Bowing up and down as you circled the sacred stone that Adam brought with him from Paradise (Appendix Adam - Paradise Lost) had become more of a dance than a sacred rite, and ribald poetry competitions were held within the sacred precinct.

Abraham's somber pilgrimage had taken on the aspect of a festival of fun and worship. The Prophet would take the fun out of the pilgrimage, but this still left the believers wary of performing rituals which, from their limited perspective, were pagan rituals. One of these rituals was the re-enactment of Hagar frantically running seven times between Safa and Marwa, names of the two mountains (hills really) near Mecca, looking for water after being abandoned there by Abraham with their son Isma'il.

Islam considers Hagar the legitimate wife of Abraham and her son by the patriarch of the Muslims and Jews his first heir. The Koran is clear on the order of birth and whom Abraham attempted to sacrifice, and that was Isma'il, a willing volunteer.

> 37:102 Then, when he attained the age of consorting with him, he said: "My son, I have seen in sleep that I am slaughtering you. See what you think." He said: "My father, do what you are commanded; you will find me, Allah willing, one of the steadfast."

Adding to the believers' uneasiness, the pagans had placed idols, which the Prophet ordered destroyed, on the hills. To sooth their troubled mind Allah sent a revelation, verse 2:158, assuring the believers that re-enacting Hagar's desperate search for water was not a sin.

There undoubtedly were other questions about emulating the believers of old, which Allah dismissed in a brilliantly formulated revelation whereby He assures the believers that if the ritual was good enough for Abraham it was good enough for them, revelation 2:130, which effectively made revelation 2:158 redundant

2:158 Surely Safa and Marwa are beacons of Allah (His Religion). He who performs the proper or the lesser pilgrimage commits no sin if he goes around them. And those who volunteer to do a good deed will find Allah Rewarding, All-Knowing.

2:130 And who would forsake the religion of Abraham except one who makes a fool of himself? We have chosen him in this world and in the Hereafter; he shall be one of the righteous.

From Curser to Pardoner of Jews

When the Prophet sought refuge in Medina he was welcomed by the Jews, not only because he believed in the one God of the Torah, but they also saw him as a man who could settle disputes between them and the Arabs of the oasis city. He became in fact the ultimate judge and jury of Medina in both secular and religious affairs.

In the post-Jesus era, the Jews were moving away from the more brutal punishments specified in the Torah, such as the stoning of adulterers. The Prophet would have none of it. He literally ruled by the Book, whether that book was the Koran or the Torah. In applying Jewish religious law he was assisted by a Jew by the name of bin Salem who had converted to Islam.

Abdullah bin Salam was a former rabbi and a respected member of the Jewish community before he converted to Islam. He became a Muslim after a short meeting with the Prophet where God's Messenger answered three fatuous questions to the rabbi's satisfaction. It was fortuitous that the angel Gabriel, whom bin Salam then considered an enemy of the Jews, had just had a conversation with the Prophet about what was on bin Salam's mind.

Narrated Anas:

Abdullah bin Salam heard the news of the arrival of Allah's Apostle (at Medina) while he was on a farm collecting its fruits. So he came to the Prophet and said, "I will ask you about three things which nobody knows unless he be a prophet. Firstly, what is the first portent of the Hour? What is the first meal of the people of Paradise? And what makes a baby look like its father or mother?"

The Prophet said, "Just now Gabriel has informed me about that."

Abdullah said, "Gabriel?"

The Prophet said, "Yes."

Abdullah said, "He, among the angels is the enemy of the Jews."

On that the Prophet recited this Holy Verse: "Whoever is an enemy to Gabriel (let him die in his fury!) for he has brought it (i.e. Qur'an) down to your heart by Allah's permission." (2:97)

Then he added, "As for the first portent of the Hour, it will be a fire that will collect the people from the East to West. And as for the first meal of the people of Paradise, it will be the caudite (i.e. extra) lobe of the fish liver. And if a man's discharge proceeded that of the woman, then the child resembles the father, and if the woman's discharge proceeded that of the man, then the child resembles the mother."

On hearing that, Abdullah said, "I testify that None has the right to be worshipped but Allah, and that you are the Apostle of Allah, O, Allah's Apostle; the Jews are liars, and if they should come to know that I have embraced Islam, they would accuse me of being a liar."

In the meantime some Jews came (to the Prophet) and he asked them, "What is Abdullah's status amongst you?"

They replied, "He is the best amongst us, and he is our chief and the son of our chief."

The Prophet said, "What would you think if Abdullah bin Salam embraced Islam?"

They replied, "May Allah protect him from this!"

Then Abdullah came out and said, "I testify that None has the right to be worshipped but Allah and that Muhammad is the Apostle of Allah."

The Jews then said, "Abdullah is the worst of us and the son of the worst of us," and disparaged him.

On that Abdullah said, "O Allah's Apostle! This is what I was afraid of!"

Bukhari 60.7

In a case brought before him which got a mention in the Koran, God's Messenger forced the Jews – over whom he had ultimate authority under the negotiated Constitution of Medina – to stick to the old ways, many of which became the news ways of the Koran.

Narrated Abdullah bin Umar:

The Jews came to Allah's Apostle and told him that a man and a woman from amongst them had committed illegal sexual intercourse.

Allah's Apostle said to them, "What do you find in the Torah (old Testament) about the legal punishment of Ar-Rajm (stoning)?"

They replied, "(But) we announce their crime and lash them."

Abdullah bin Salam said, "You are telling a lie; Torah contains the order of Rajm."

They brought and opened the Torah and one of them solaced [placed] his hand on the Verse of Rajm and read the verses preceding and following it.

Abdullah bin Salam said to him, "Lift your hand." When he lifted his hand, the Verse of Rajm was written there.

They said, "Muhammad has told the truth; the Torah has the Verse of Rajm."

The Prophet then gave the order that both of them should be stoned to death.

(Abdullah bin Umar said, "I saw the man leaning over the woman to shelter her from the stones.")

Bukhari 56.829.

What they tried to concealed from His Messenger infuriated Allah, as evident in revelation 2:159, but perhaps only for a moment. Revelation 2:160 does not so much annulled revelation 2:159 as attenuate Allah's anger against the Jews, if only for the time being.

2:159 Those (the Jews) who conceal the clear proofs and guidance We sent down, after making them clear to mankind in the Book (the Torah), shall be cursed by Allah and the cursers.

2:160 Except those who repent, mend their ways and reveal [the truth which they had concealed]; these I shall pardon. I am the Pardoner, the Merciful.

Providing for a Widow

2:234 As for those of you who die leaving wives behind, their wives should observe a waiting period (during this period they should stay away from men) of four months and ten days. When they have completed that period you incur no offence on account of what they may do to themselves (such as adorning themselves or looking out for suitors) in a lawful manner. Allah has knowledge of what you do.

2:240 Those of you who die leaving wives behind should bequeath to them a year's provision without turning [them] out (from their homes). If however, they leave [their homes], then you (the relatives of the dead) incur no offence for what they do in a rightful way to themselves. Allah is Mighty, Wise.

Having the deceased in the abrogating revelation leave a year's provision to his widows is welcomed and will stand them in good staid when they are forced to leave their deceased husband's home (Islamic law recognizes the husband as the sole proprietor of the family home) and his relatives move in.

Dying a Muslim by Doing What a Muslim Does

It goes without saying that you should not die except as a Muslim. If you do as a Muslim does, as explained in verse 64:16 which Allah sent to replace revelation 3:102, you will die a believer, making the revealed truth it replaces unnecessary.

3:102 O believers fear Allah as He should be feared, and do not die except as Muslims.

64:16 So, fear Allah as much as you can, listen, obey and spend freely (in the Cause of Allah). That is best for you. He who is guarded against the avarice of his soul – those are the prosperous.

No More Mr. Nice Guy II

There was a time when Allah would have forgiven a heretic who returned to the fold if asked to do so by His Messenger.

4:64 We have not sent forth a Messenger, but that he may be obeyed by Allah's Leave. And had they, having wronged themselves, come to you and asked for Allah's Forgiveness and the Messenger had asked forgiveness for them, then they would have found Allah All-Forgiving, Merciful.

9:80 Ask forgiveness for them or do not ask forgiveness for them. If you ask forgiveness for them seventy times, Allah will not forgive them; because they disbelieve in Allah and His Messenger. Allah does not guide the sinful people.

The last unbelievers Allah would forgive, as a favour to His favourite and greatest Messenger, were the Prophet's mother and father (Appendix Allah's Mercy).

Indoctrination and War

> Allah's Apostle said, "I have been sent with the shortest expressions bearing the widest meanings, and I have been made victorious with terror ..."
>
> *Bukhari 52.220*

As the believers made progress is subjugating, through the force of arms and terror the non-Muslims of the Peninsula and more warriors joined the Muslims, if only to indulge in the general plunder of the unbelievers' property, indoctrination of these new recruits into the new religion took on a new urgency.

4:71 O believers, be on your guard; so march in detachments or march altogether.

9:122 The believers should not all go to war. Why doesn't a company from each group go forth to instruct themselves in religion and admonish their people (those who go to war) when they return, that perchance, they may beware.

Allah expected some of the believers to stay behind for another strategic reason, anticipating a tactic used today in the modern propaganda wars, that of spreading misinformation or what is commonly referred to as *War's First Casualty*, the truth.

> 4:72 Indeed, among you is one who will stay behind, so that if a disaster befalls you, he will say: "Allah has favoured me, since I have not been a martyr with them."
>
> 4:73 If, however, a bounty from God comes to you, he will say, as though there was no friendship between you and him: "Would that I had been with them; then I would have won a great victory."

A Blood-Money Conundrum I

Payments in blood and chattel and retaliation in kind are central concepts in Islam. (Appendix Cain and Abel) The price was obliquely set by Allah during the Prophet's grandfather's lifetime.

Abd al-Muttalib, in another variation of the story of Abraham and Isaac and the thwarted immolation, had promised Allah to sacrifice his tenth son if He gave him ten male heirs. When the time came for al-Muttalib to keep his promise, he consulted a dervish to find out if he could fulfil his promise to God in some other manner that did not involve killing his tenth son, Abdullah, who was destined to be God's Messenger's father.

The dervish the Prophet's grandfather consulted was no ordinary soothsayer; he was a dervish with jinns (Appendix The Jinn - Introduction) in his employ who specialized in eavesdropping on Allah's conversations with his angels and on the angels talking among themselves. They would fly as close as possible to the lowest of the seven levels of heaven, the one closest to the earth, dogging rocks thrown by the angels to keep them away, to find out what Allah had to say about was happening down below.

To try to answer his client's question, the dervish sent his jinns to eavesdrop on God's conversation. One reported that Allah, in a conversation with an angel, had indicated that he would be happy with a sacrifice of camels. But how many camels! The dervish then threw some dice (bone fragments of some type according to Virgil Gheorghiu author of La vie de Mahomet) to *divine* an answer.

In his assessment of the way the fragments scattered, which may not have been unlike reading tea leaves, the dervish said that they indicated that God would be satisfied with a payment of one hundred camels. This is the price the Prophet reminded the faithful in his Last Khutba i.e. last sermon (Appendix The Prophet's Last Sermon) shortly before he died, that Allah had set as the blood-payment to the family or clan of the deceased for a non-premeditated homicide – what our legal system defines as the crime of manslaughter.

> And intentional murder shall be punished according to talion law; where the murderess intention is not clear and the victim is killed using a club or a stone it will cost the perpetrator one hundred camels as blood money. Whoever demands more is a man from the time of ignorance. (*Hamidullah*)

What part of revelation 4:92 is abrogated by revelation 9:1, if any, we cannot say with certainty; but we can be sure it is not the portion about blood-money. This conclusion is based on the Prophet, in his last khutba, restating Allah's position on blood-money.

4:92 It is not given to a believer to kill another believer except by mistake; and he who kills a believer by mistake should free a slave who is a believer and pay blood-money to his relatives, unless they remit it as alms. If he happens to belong to a people who are your enemies, but he is a believer, then you should free a believing slave. If he belongs to a people bound to you by compact, then blood-money should be paid to his relatives and a believing slave should be freed. As for him who has not the means, he should fast for two consecutive months, as a penance from Allah. Allah is All-Knowing, Wise!

9:1 This is immunity from Allah and His Messenger to those idolaters with whom you made compacts.

From Killing Ten to Killing Two

When Allah said that one believer could overcome ten armed unbelievers, battles were very much decided in man-to-man combat with swords and spears. Today, a believer with a bomb can easily slaughter ten unbelievers. Then, it was extremely unrealistic to expect one believer to triumph over ten unbelievers bent on making him a martyr.

Knowing the future and the improvements in body weaponry e.g. the suicide vest that would make it child's play, pun intended, for one believer to do away, in a flash of fire and shrapnel, with scores of Allah's real and imaginary enemies, why did Allah revise downward His per capita estimate as to how many unbelievers a believer could kill. Had He stuck to His original estimate, today He might be considered both a god and a visionary by more than the credulous.

8:65 O Prophet, urge the believers to fight. If there are twenty steadfast men among you, they will defeat two hundred; and if there are a hundred, they will defeat a thousand of the unbelievers, because they are a people who do not understand.

8:66 Now Allah has lightened your burden; He knows that there is a weakness in you. So, if there are a hundred steadfast men among you, they will overcome two hundred; and if there are a thousand men among you, they will overcome two thousand, by Allah's Leave. Allah is with the steadfast.

Entering a House Other Than Your Own

Allah is often quick, as a god should be, to change His mind when realizing that what He revealed as a sacred immutable truth minutes, hours, days even months earlier was not realistic, such as demanding that you always ask permission to enter a house other than your own. What about an empty house which circumstances require you enter?

24:27 O believers, do not enter houses other than your own before you ask leave and greet their occupants. This is better for you, that perchance you may remember well.

24:29 It is no offence for you to enter uninhabited houses in which you have some means of enjoyment. Allah knows what you reveal and what you conceal.

Marriage is Good, Adultery Bad

It is not clear if revelation 24:32 is an abrogating revelation or simply there to emphasize Allah's preference for married people.

24:3 The adulterer shall marry none but an adulteress or an idolatress; and the adulteress none shall marry her but an adulterer or idolater. That has been forbidden the believers.

24:32 Encourage the unmarried among you and the righteous among your servants and maids to marry. If they are poor, Allah will enrich them from His Bounty. Allah is All-Embracing, All-Knowing.

Depending on how quickly Allah changed His mind (if He actually did) as to whom an adulteress and adulterer could marry, an adulterous couple in love, if they were willing to endure a good whipping, would be automatically divorced and available to marry each other.

> 24:2 The adulteress and the adulterer, whip each one of them a hundred lashes; and let no pity move you in Allah's religion, regarding them; if you believe in Allah and the Hereafter. And let a group of believers witness their punishment.

An adulteress might have also been able to get out of an abusive relationship without having to pay a ransom.

> 2:229 Divorce may be pronounced twice. Then they (women) are to be retained in a rightful manner or released with kindness. And it is unlawful for you [men] to take back anything of what you have given them unless both parties fear that they cannot comply with Allah's Bounds (by obeying His commands). If you fear that they cannot do that, then it is no offence if the woman ransoms herself [pays money to be set free]. Those are the bounds set by Allah. Do not transgress them. Those who transgress the bounds set by Allah are the wrongdoers.

My list of abrogated verses does not include another revelation about the punishment of adulteresses where Allah has to think about a suitable penance, which verse 24:2 would appear to abrogate.

> 4:15 As for those of your women who commit adultery, call four witnesses from your own against them; and if they testify then detain them in the houses till death overtakes them or Allah opens another way for them.

Some scholars maintain that both revealed truths 24:3 and 4:15 were abrogated by what is known as the *Lost Verse* (Appendix Stoning), an alleged revelation in which Allah finally settles on stoning as the most appropriate punishment for an adulteress.

From Whipping to Pardoning Slanderers of Chaste Women

24:4 Those who accuse chaste women, then cannot bring four witnesses, whip them eighty lashes, and do not ever accept their testimony. For those are the wicked sinners.

24:5 Except for those who repent afterwards and mend their ways. For Allah is surely All-Forgiving, Merciful.

Revelation 24:4 was probably sent in the heat of the moment, the heat being generated by accusations that the Prophet's child-bride had committed adultery. Aisha got lost in the desert one evening and was returned to her husband the next day by the young man who found her. Needless to say, rumors, which severely distressed God's Messenger, ran rampant, prompting Allah to issue a warning to those who would slander the wife of his greatest and last spokesperson. You may ignore the fact that the abrogated and abrogating verses come after Allah's tirade in the following verses against those who would accuse Aisha of betraying her husband. Even within surahs, order of precedence is ignored. Past, present and future is for mortals.

> 24:11 Those who spread the slander (against Aisha, wife of the Prophet, according to the commentators) are a band of you. Do not reckon it an evil for you; rather it is a good thing for you. Every one of them will be credited with the sin he has earned, and he who bore the brunt of it shall have a terrible punishment.
>
> 24:12 Would that the believers, men and women, when you heard it (the slander) had though well of themselves saying: "This is manifest slander!"
>
> 24:13 And would that they had brought forth four witnesses [to vouch for it]! But since they did not bring any witnesses, those are, in Allah's sight, the real liars.

The Prophet's son-in-law, Ali, even suggested that Aisha be stoned, telling his father-in-law that "Allah has not placed any limits on the choice of a wife. They are plentiful." After Allah calmed down, perhaps after realizing that His Messenger's son-in-law might have to be whipped, He communicated to the angel Gabriel, who passed it on to the Prophet, that, on second thought, if an accuser of chase women repented, he should not be whipped.

Generalities about a Woman's Finery

When you spot a middle-aged or older female believer going about her business still draped in that dark tent-like garment, she is simply complying with Allah's recommendation "that to refrain" from removing cumbersome layers of clothing is better, even if no finery is exhibited in doing so. For women who are still young enough to bear children, even removing an outer garment is out of the question. Again, revelation 24:60 is not a verse that abrogates, so much as adds to what Allah decreed post-pubescent females should wear and how they should behave if males are in the vicinity.

24:31 And tell the believing women to cast down their eyes and guard their private parts and not show their finery, except the outward part of it. And let them drape their bosoms with their veils and not show their finery, except to their husbands, their fathers, their husbands' fathers, their sons, the sons of their husbands, their brothers, the sons of their brothers, the sons of their sisters, their women, their maid-servants, the men-followers who have no sexual desire, or infants who have no knowledge of women's sexual parts yet. Let them, also, not stamp their feet, so that what they have concealed of their finery might be known. Repent to Allah, all of you, O believers, that perchance you may prosper.

24:60 Those women who are past child-bearing and have no hope of marriage are not at fault if they take off their outer garments, not exhibiting any finery; but to refrain is better for them. Allah is All-Hearing, All-Knowing.

Slave-Girls and Children Close By and You're Naked

24:58 O believers, let those your right hands possess (slaves and maid-servants) and those who have not reached the age of puberty ask your leave three times: (to attend to you or approach you) before the dawn prayer, when you put off your clothes at noon and after the evening prayer. These are three occasions of nudity for you; after which you are or they are not at fault, if you approach each other. That is how Allah makes clear His signs to you. Allah is All-Knowing, Wise.

24:59 And when your children reach puberty, let them ask leave, as those who came before them asked leave. That is how Allah makes clear His Signs to you. Allah is All-Knowing, Wise.

Revelation 25:58 appears to sanction intimacy between a slave-owner and his slave-girls and an employer and an employee i.e. maid if after having seen their employer/owner naked three times they can't resist wanting to get closer. There is of course no hint of sanctioned impropriety in the alleged abrogating revelation which extends the requirement to ask for leave to post-pubescent children before approaching their father, one has to assume when he is getting ready for prayer.

Wives for the Messenger

Pre-Islamic Arabs made no distinction between adopted and natural-born sons until Allah decreed a distinction so that His Messenger could marry his adopted son's wife.

> 33:4 Allah did not create two hearts within the breast of any man; and He did not make your wives, whom you compare to your mothers' backs; and He did not make your [adopted] sons your sons in fact. That is your own claim, by your words of mouth. Allah speaks the truth and He guides to the Right Path.

God's Messenger walked in on his daughter-in-law Zaynab when she was almost naked and he just had to have her. His adopted son divorced her so that the man he considered his father could marry her. Allah quickly confirmed the righteous of what Zayd had done, and what the Prophet did after.

> 33:37 And [remember] when you said to him whom Allah favoured and you favoured: (this is addressed to Zayd regarding his wife Zaynab) "Hold on to your wife and fear Allah", while you concealed within yourself what Allah would reveal and feared other men, whereas Allah had a better right to be feared by you. Then, when Zayd had

satisfied his desire for her, We gave her to you in marriage; so that the believers should not be at fault, regarding the wives of their adopted sons, once they have satisfied their desire for them. For Allah's Command must be accomplished.

Even Aisha was taken aback, telling her husband that when it came to his accumulation of bed-partners "I feel that your Lord hastens in fulfilling your wishes and desires." Bukhari 60.675. This may have been the sentiment of many for Allah to send down a revelation telling His Messenger that enough was enough, revelation 33:52 (another revelation nullified by a higher number verse), which He later abrogated replacing it with a reveal truth, revelation 33:50, which confirmed the double-standard when it came to women an ordinary believer and His Messenger could marry.

33:52 Thereafter, other women are not lawful to you, nor is substituting other wives for them, even if you admire their beauty, except for what your right hand owns. Allah is Watchful over everything.	33:50 O Prophet, we have made lawful, for you, your wives, whose dowry you have paid, what your right hand owns (slave-girls) out of the spoils of war that Allah gave you, the daughters of your paternal uncles, the daughters of your paternal aunts, the daughters of your maternal uncles, the daughters of your maternal aunts who emigrated with you, and any believing woman who gives herself freely to the Prophet, if the Prophet desires to marry her, granted exclusively to you, but not the believers. We know what We have prescribed for them regarding their wives and what their right hands own, so that you may not be at fault. Allah is All-Forgiving, Merciful.

It is one of the Koran's most confounding mysteries – if you don't believe that a man was using god to get women into his bed – that a god, in a book meant to be the ultimate guide for mankind as to how to live a god-fearing life, spent so much time on the sex life of just one man? If that sex life was to be held up as an example to the faithful, then perhaps it would have its place in such as book, but as an exception to Allah's rules for the ordinary believer? I don't think so.

In seeking to please His Messenger when it came to whom he could have intimate relations with, Allah did a tremendous disservice to Muslim orphan boys, a disservice which is felt to this day. The reveal truths changing the relationship between adopted sons and their surrogate parent so that God's Messenger could add his daughter-in-law Zaynab to his collection of wives, concubines and slave-girls have been interpreted to mean that Islam is against Western style adoption, resulting in an untold number of children in the Islamic world who have no one to call father.

The Prophet as Savior

At first glance 48:2 leaves you wondering, like so many revelations, as to why and what is it abrogating. Often the answer is in the preceding or following revelation, in this instance it is the revelations (in italics) that introduce the abrogated verse.

39:11 Say: "I have been commanded to worship Allah, professing to Him the religion sincerely.

39:12 "And I have been commanded to be the first of those who submit."

39:13 Say: "I fear if I disobey my Lord, the punishment of a great Day."

48:2 That Allah may forgive you your former and your later sins, and complete His Blessing upon you and lead you onto a straight path;

Jesus (Appendix Jesus) was sent to do what needed to be done so his followers would be saved, and so it would seem was the Prophet.

They Also Carry Allah's Throne

Angels (Appendix Angels) do more than just praise the Lord and ask for forgiveness for the believers, as the verse which abrogates a portion of 42:5 makes clear.

42:5 *The heavens are almost rent asunder above them;* while the angels proclaim the praise of their Lord and ask forgiveness for those on earth. Lo, Allah is truly the All-Forgiving, The Merciful!

40:7 Those who carry the Throne and those around it proclaim the praise of their Lord, believe in Him and ask forgiveness for the believers: "Lord, You have encompassed everything in mercy and knowledge; so forgive those who have repented and followed your Path, and guard them against the punishment of Hell.

Wages for the Messenger

Verse 42:23 is a Meccan verse as is its abrogator. However, revelation 42:23 may have been received during the time that the Prophet's first wife Khadijah was still solvent and therefore he could afford to preach for nothing. Khadijah, a wealthy older Meccan woman hired the good-looking trader – and later married (her third, his first) the allegedly illiterate young man – to accompany her caravans to and from Damascus.

In asking for a voluntary wage in the revelation that abrogates the verse about asking for no payment for the Message he is delivering,

Allah communicates to His Messenger to say that He will be watching. Again, ignore the sequence which appears to have an earlier revelation abrogate a future revelation, a jumble which was kindly described by Justin Wintle author of History of Islam as "jumping from one subject to another in a sort of unfurling stream of supra-consciousness" i.e. a consciousness or awareness that is beyond our understanding.

42:23 Say: (O Muhammad) "I ask you no reward for it (this message, *Muhammad Assad*) except kinship towards kinsmen." Whoever performs a good deed, We shall increase its goodness. Allah is truly All-Forgiving, Thankful.

34:47 Say: "Whatever wage I asked you for is yours [to give]. My wage is with Allah and He is a witness of everything."

The Reward of Beneficence

53:39 And that man will only earn what he strives for;

52:21 And those who have believed and their progeny followed them in belief, We shall join their progeny to them. We shall not deprive them of any of their work; every man shall be bound by what he has earned.

What men will earn is well documented in the Koran, the most talked about being Allah's artificial creation, female lookalikes skilled in the art of pleasing any man's most intimate desires, the famous houris.

56:22 And wide-eyed houris,

56:23 Like hidden pearls;

56:24 As a reward for what they used to do.

44:54 Thus it will be; and we gave them wide-eyed houris in marriage.

52:20: Reclining on ranged couches, and We shall wed them to wide-eyed houris.

Not to be overlooked are blushing maidens, an extraordinary bounty you cannot deny:

55:56 Therein are maidens lowering their glances and they have not been touched, before them by any man or jinn.

55:57 So, which of your Lord's Bounties do you both (Jinn and humans) deny?

55:58 They are like rubies and coral.

55:59 So, which of your Lord's Bounties do you both (Jinn and humans) deny?

55:60 Shall the reward of beneficence be other than beneficence?

But what about women, what is in it for them for doing good? This is where abrogating revelation 52:21 comes in handy as demonstrated in a response to a question from a prospective female martyr about the rewards a female jihadist can expect from Allah for fighting and dying to extend his dominion on earth? According to David Cook, such a question was asked on a Hamas website by a prospective female suicide bomber; would she get the equivalent of the male suicide bombers who are promised a "fairly extensive harem of women in return for martyrdom."

> [Question] I wanted to ask: what is the reward of a female martyr who performs a martyrdom operation; does she marry 72 of the houris?
>
> [Answer] ... the female martyr gains the same rewards as does the male, with the exception of this one aspect [the houris], so that the female martyr will be with the same husband with whom she dies. "And those who have believed and their progeny, followed them in belief. We shall join their progeny to them. We shall not deprive them of any of their work; every man shall be bound by what he has earned" [52:21]. The one who is martyred and has no husband will be married to one of the people of Paradise.

David Cook, Understanding Jihad, p.146

For the Prophet Only

Abrogating revelation 58:13 is another of those revealed truths that are for God's Messenger only and that have no obvious relevance once he died.

58:12 O believers, if you converse privately with the Messenger, then tender a free offering before your secret conversing. That is better for you and purer; but if you do not have the means, then Allah is All-Forgiving, Merciful.

58:13 Do you dread to make free offerings before your private converse? If you do not do so and Allah pardons you, then perform the prayer, give the alms and obey Allah and His Messenger. Allah is Aware of what you do.

Perhaps the abrogating revelation is meant to apply to the Prophets' successors as leader of the believers the so-called caliphs; if not, it's simply another one of those revelations with whom Allah favoured His favourite and greatest spokesperson and which are meant to demonstrate the esteem in which He was held during his time in the here-and-now.

Forgive and Forget is Not Allah's Way

Allah does not forgive and forget, and neither should the believers if they don't want Him to consider them wrongdoers and all the awful things that entails, including roasting in Hell for an eternity.

60:8 Allah does not forbid you, regarding those who did not fight you and did not drive you out of your homes, to be generous to them and deal with them justly. Allah surely loves the just.

60:9 Allah only forbids you, regarding those who fought you in religion and drove you out of your homes and assisted in driving you out, to take them for friends. Those who take them for friends are, indeed, the wrongdoers. Allah is Aware of what you do.

That Sound You Hear

The Prophet received communications from God at all hours of the night and day, when he may have not always worn the same garment. This may explain Allah's abrogation of revelation 73:1 about how His Messenger was attired when Gabriel delivered the *latest* from on High.

73:1 O enwrapped one (that is Muhammad, who used to be 'wrapped up' when the Koran was imparted to him by the Angel Gabriel),

73:2 Keep vigil throughout the night, except for a little while;

73:3 Half of it, or a little less;

73:4 Or add a little thereto and chant the Qur'an loudly.

It Was Not a Weighty Message After All

73:5 Indeed, We shall deliver unto you a weighty discourse.

4:28 Allah wishes to lighten your burden; for man was created weak.

Wishing Won't Make It So

73:19 This is truly a reminder (*the Qur'an*); so that he who wishes may follow unto his Lord a path.

76:30 Yet, you do not wish unless Allah wishes. Allah is truly All-Knowing and Wise.

80:12 Whoever wishes will remember it (*the Qur'an*);

81:29 But you will not wish unless Allah, the Lord of the Worlds, wishes.

73:19 This is truly a

76:30 Yet, you do not wish unless

reminder (*the Qur'an*); so that he who wishes may follow unto his Lord a path.

Allah wishes. Allah is truly All-Knowing and Wise.

81:28 To whoever of you who wishes to reform their ways.

81:29 But you will not wish unless Allah, the Lord of the Worlds, wishes.

Mouthing the Koran Was Not Good Enough

The Prophet or perhaps the believers may have initially misunderstood what was being asked of them.

75:16 Do not wag your tongue with it (the Qur'an) to hurry on with it.

87:6 We shall make you recite; so you will not forget;

Many Abrogating One

A Blood-Money Conundrum II

2:178 O believers, retaliation for the slain is prescribed for you; a free [man] for a free [man], a slave for a slave and a female for a female. But if he is pardoned by his brother (the aggrieved), usage should be followed (capital punishment would be replaced by blood-money) and he should pay him (the aggrieved) liberally and kindly. This is remission and mercy from your Lord. He who transgresses after that will have a painful punishment.

5:45 And We prescribed to them therein (the Torah) that a life for a life, an eye for an eye, a nose for a nose, an ear for an ear, a tooth for a tooth, and for wounds retaliation; but whoever forgoes it charitably, it will be an atonement for him. Whoever does not judge according to what Allah has revealed, those are the evildoers!

17:33 Do not kill the soul which Allah has forbidden except for a just cause. Whoever is killed unjustly, We have given his heir the power [to demand satisfaction]; but let him not exceed the limit in slaying, for he will be the victor.

The above abrogated verse, revelation 2:178 is from a Medinan surah and one of its nullifiers, verse 17:33, is from a Meccan surah. How is this possible, a revelation from the pass abrogating a revelation from the future? Gods work in mysterious ways and Allah is no exception, and in abrogating revelation 2:178 He is doubly so.

None of the abrogating revelations mention the payment of blood money. This should be an indication that the payment of blood-money sanctioned in the abrogated revelation is no longer valid (see explanation in *A Blood-Money Conundrum I* for why this is not the case).

Wills and Testaments

Pre-Islamic wills allowed the Prophet's first wife to be wealthy in her own right and not be dependent on any man for her sustenance. She probably was the last Muslim female to benefit from the pre-Islamic rules, or lack thereof, governing wills.

Initially, Allah was comfortable with the well-established practice of a person making a will in which he or she disposed of their wealth as they saw fit. In fact, He insisted on it in abrogated revelation 2:180, even if leaving something for the wives is not mentioned.

In setting rules governing the disposition of an "estate" in revelations which abrogate verse 2:180, Allah mentions females, but it is not to their advantage, unless, like many apologist for Islam such as Karen Armstrong, you argue that daughters were now guaranteed at least a share of the wealth, even if that share could never be more than half of a brother's bequest.

2:180 It is prescribed for you that when death is imminent for one of you and he leaves wealth, he should equitably make a testament in favour of the parents and the near of kin. This in incumbent upon the righteous.

4:7 Men should have a share of what parents and kinsmen leave behind; and women a share of what parents and kinsmen leave, whether big or small, as an obligatory portion.

4:11 Allah commands you, with respect to your children, that the male shall inherit the equivalent of the share of two females. If there be more than two females, then they should receive two-thirds of what he (the deceased father) leaves; but if there is only one female, she is entitled to one-half. To each of his parents, one-sixth of what he leaves, if he has any children; but if he has no children, then his parents will inherit him, the mother receiving one third. But if he has any brothers, then his mother receives one-sixth, after any will he had made or any debt he had incurred [is taken care of] Your fathers and sons – you know not who of them is of greater advantage to you. This is a law from Allah; Allah surely is All-Knowing, Forbearing.

Allah's final revealed truths as to the disposition of an inheritance where He decides who gets what, inaugurated a vicious circle of self-serving regulations which favoured men at women's expense and ensured that believing females to survive in this world will have to depend on the generosity of God's preferred sex, and for a share of the Hereafter, to be thankful for getting anything at all.

Narrated Ibn Abbas:

The Prophet said: "I was shown the Hell-fire and that the majority of its dwellers were women who were ungrateful."

It was asked, "Do they disbelieve in Allah?" (or are they ungrateful to Allah?)

He replied, "They are ungrateful to their husbands and are ungrateful for the favors and the good (charitable deeds) done to them."

Bukhari 2.28

Intoxicants

2:219 They ask you about wine and gambling, say: "In both there is great sin and some benefit for people. But the sin is greater than the benefit." And they ask you about what they should spend, say: "What you can spare." Thus Allah makes clear to you His Revelations so that you may reflect.

4:43 O believers, do not approach prayer while you are drunk, until you know what you say; nor when you are unclean – unless you are on a journey – until you have washed yourselves. And if you are sick or on a journey, or if anyone of you has relieved himself, or you have touched women and could not find water, you might rub yourself with clean earth, wiping you faces and hands with it. Allah is indeed All Pardoning, All-Forgiving.

5:90 O believers, wine, gambling, idols and divining arrows are an abomination of the Devil's doing; so avoid them that perchance you may prosper!

9:103 Take of their wealth voluntary alms to purify and cleanse them therewith; and pray for them, for your prayers are a source of tranquility for them. Allah is All-Hearing, All-Knowing.

Revealed truth 4:43 is special in that scholars have determined that it, in turn, has been abrogated by revealed truth 5:90. Also, revealed truth 5:90 abrogates another revelation where Allah is very much tolerant of wine drinkers.

16:67 And from the fruits of palms and vines, you get wine and fair provision. Surely, there is in that a sign to a people who understand.

Revelation 2:219 contains two disparate revealed truths. This is not that unusual. My favorite incongruent two-revealed-truths revelation is verse 2:189 where Allah begins by telling His Messenger what to say when asked about the timing of the pilgrimage to Mecca and concludes with a warning about entering a house via the back door.

2:189 They ask you about the crescents (the new moons) say: "They are times fixed for mankind and for the pilgrimage." It is not righteousness to enter houses from the back; but the righteous is he who fears Allah. Enter then the houses by their front doors; and fear Allah that you may prosper.

The two transient revealed truths in revelation 2:219 are abrogated by separate revelations. Verse 9:103 abrogates the second revealed, now obsolete, truth which begins with "And they ask you about what they should spend ..."

You may remember revelation 9:103 as abrogating revelation 2:3 (section *Charity Becomes a Tax*). Here, 9:103 does more or less the same thing, nullifying a revelation from God where He demonstrates some flexibility as to how believers spend their wealth, with one where He doesn't. Allah may have been less dogmatic early on when it came to alcoholic beverages, but perhaps not His Messenger, if the beating he demanded be administered to a drunk occurred before Allah informed His Messenger, in revelation 5:90, of His hardened attitudes towards intoxicants.

Narrated Abu Salama:

> Abu Huraira said, "A man who drank wine was brought to the Prophet. The Prophet said, 'Beat him!'"
>
> Abu Huraira added, "So some of us beat him with our hands, and some with their shoes, and some with their garments (by twisting it) like a lash, and then when we finished, someone said to him, 'May Allah disgrace you!' On that the Prophet said, 'Do not say so, for you are helping Satan to overpower him.'"
>
> *Bukhari 81.768*

That alcohol is a concoction of Satin which he uses to subjugate the believers is not mentioned in revelation 2:219; an oversight which Allah may also have wanted to remedy in sending revelation 5:90 as a replacement.

When the Prophet and his believers-on-the-run first settled in Medina, it is obvious from the first short-lived revealed truth of revelation 2:219 that Allah was much more tolerant of wine drinkers. This all changed after a battle which the believers almost lost. Allah may have blamed the consumption of alcohol for the believers ignoring the Prophet's instruction at the battle of Uhud not to be distracted by the booty – in this instance, Meccan females loitering by a caravan – until the battle was won.

Narrated Anas:

> I used to offer alcoholic drinks to the people at the residence of Abu Talha. Then the order of prohibiting alcoholic drinks was revealed, and the Prophet ordered somebody to announce that.
>
> Abu Talha said to me, "Go out and see what this voice (this announcement) is."

I went out and (on coming back) said, "This is somebody announcing that alcoholic beverages have been prohibited."

Abu Talha said to me, "Go and spill it (i.e. the wine)," Then it (alcoholic drinks) was seen flowing through the streets of Medina. At that time the wine was Al-Fadikh.

The people said, "Some people (Muslims) were killed (during the battle of Uhud) while wine was in their stomachs."

So Allah revealed: "On those who believe and do good deeds there is no blame for what they ate (in the past)." (5:93)

Bukhari 60.144

I left the first abrogation, in numerical order, for last as I have no clue as to why our eminent medieval scholars included it here as an abrogator of verse 2:219 – not that it does not contain stuff that a believer needs to know. But that is not the point.

The Divorce Ransom and Marriage to an Impotent Man

2:228 Divorced women should keep away from men for three menstrual periods. And it is not lawful for them to conceal that which Allah has created in their wombs, if they truly believe in Allah and the Last Day. Their husbands have the right in the meantime to take them back, should they seek reconciliation; and women have rights equal to what is incumbent upon them according to what is just, although men are one degree above them (what is meant here is that the men have a superior authority). Allah is Mighty, Wise.

2:229 Divorce may be pronounced twice. Then they (women) are to be retained in a rightful manner or released with kindness. And it is unlawful for you [men] to take back anything of what you have given them unless both parties fear that they cannot comply with Allah's Bounds (by obeying His commands). If you fear that they cannot do that, then it is no offence if the woman ransoms herself [pays money to be set free]. Those are the bounds set by Allah. Do not transgress them. Those who transgress the bounds set by Allah are the wrongdoers.

2:230 If he divorces her, she shall not be lawful to him again until she has married another husband. If the latter divorces her, then it is no offence if they go back to each other, if they both think that they shall keep within Allah's Bounds. Those are Allah's Bounds which He makes clear to men who have knowledge.

There is no mention in the two verses abrogating revelation 2:228 that men are no longer superior to women by at least one degree, therefore it is safe to assume that that revealed truth is still an immutable fact. We also have the Prophet's declaration during his last sermon that women are like prisoners in their husband's or father's house. A prisoner is not the equal of her jailer.

> Treat the women kindly, for verily, they are like prisoners in your house and are incapable of looking after themselves ...

From the Prophet's last sermon

If there is any doubt that, like His Messenger, Allah considers wives prisoners in their husband's home it is the abrogating revelation where Allah reveals that a wife can get out of a marriage if she pays a ransom that is acceptable to her husband, his keeping her dowry being the most common. However, if a divorcee is unfortunate enough to then marry an impotent man, no amount of money can get her out of that jail.

Narrated Ikrima:

Rifa'a divorced his wife whereupon Abdur-Rahman bin Az-Zubair Al-Qurazi married her.

Aisha said that the lady (came), wearing a green veil (and complained to her (Aisha) of her husband and showed her a green spot on her skin caused by beating).

It was the habit of ladies to support each other, so when Allah's Apostle came, Aisha said, "I have not seen any women suffering as much as the believing women. Look! Her skin is greener than her clothes!"

When Abdur-Rahman heard that his wife had gone to the Prophet, he came with his two sons from another wife.

She said, "By Allah! I have done no wrong to him but he is impotent and is as useless to me as this," holding and showing the fringe of her garment.

Abdur-Rahman said, "By Allah, O Allah's Apostle! She has told a lie! I am very strong and can satisfy her but she is disobedient and wants to go back to Rifa'a."

Allah's Apostle said, to her, "If that is your intention, then know that it is unlawful for you to remarry Rifa'a unless Abdur-Rahman has had sexual intercourse with you."

Then the Prophet saw two boys with Abdur-Rahman and asked (him), "Are these your sons?"

On that Abdu-Rahman said, "Yes."

The Prophet said, "You claim what you claim (i.e. that he is impotent)? But by Allah, these boys resemble him as a crow resembles a crow,"

Bukhari 72.715

He Said, She Said.

First it was his swearing four times that he was telling the truth and her swearing four times that he was a liar that warded off the punishment, then Allah upped the ante, revelations 24:7 and 24:9, the acrimonious couple were now to swear a fifth time about the truthfulness of their respective allegations and whoever was lying was in for a very bad time. If the husband lied a fifth time about seeing his wife being intimate with another man, he was cursed by Allah. If a wife lied a fifth time about seeing her husband having sex with a woman to whom he was not married, she incurred the Wrath of Allah. As to the liar who got the worse of Allah's displeasure, I would hazard the wife; you can overcome the misfortunes that come with being cursed, but you cannot escape the Wrath of Allah.

24:6 And those who accuse their wives and have no witnesses except themselves, the testimony of one of them shall be to swear by Allah four times that he is truthful.

24:7 The fifth time shall be Allah's Curse on him if he is a liar.

24:8 ...

24:9 And the fifth time will be that Allah's Wrath be upon her, if he (her husband) is truthful.

Gabriel interrupted the Prophet's interrogation of a gutsy woman accused of having intercourse with a man other than her lawfully wedded husband to communicate to God's Messenger the addition of the fifth oath and the curse that came with it, but not before her husband pointed out to the Prophet the absurdity of seeking four people to observe his wife having sex with another man.

Narrated Ibn Abbas:

Hilal bin Umaiya accused his wife of committing illegal sexual intercourse with Sharik bin Sahma and filed the case before the Prophet.

The Prophet said (to Hilal), "Either you bring forth a proof (four witnesses) or you will receive the legal punishment (lashes) on your back."

Hilal said, "O Allah's Apostle! If anyone of us saw a man over his wife, would he go to seek after witnesses?"

The Prophet kept on saying, "Either you bring forth the witnesses or you will receive the legal punishment (lashes) on your back."

Hilal then said, "By Him Who sent you with the Truth, I am telling the truth and Allah will reveal to you what will save my back from legal punishment."

Then Gabriel came down and revealed to him: 'As for those who accuse their wives...' (24:6-9)

The Prophet recited it till he reached: '... (her accuser) is telling the truth.'

Then the Prophet left and sent for the woman, and Hilal went (and brought) her and then took the oaths (confirming the claim).

The Prophet was saying, "Allah knows that one of you is a liar, so will any of you repent?"

Then the woman got up and took the oaths and when she was going to take the fifth one, the people stopped her and said, "It (the fifth oath) will definitely bring Allah's curse on you (if you are guilty)."

So she hesitated and recoiled (from taking the oath) so much that we thought that she would withdraw her denial. But then she said, "I will not dishonor my family all through these days," and carried on (the process of taking oaths).

The Prophet then said, "Watch her; if she delivers a black-eyed child with big hips and fat shins then it is Sharik bin Sahma's child."

Later she delivered a child of that description. So the Prophet said, "If the case was not settled by Allah's Law, I would punish her severely."

Bukhari 60.271

Her husband might have gotten whipped if he had been caught in a lie, but not his wife. By punishing "her severely", the Prophet meant having her stoned to death, as were most, if not all of the women who were judged guilty of adultery by the man the believers revere as the Prophet of Mercy, an oxymoron where the defenceless were concerned.

God's Messenger began to be referred to as the Prophet of Mercy after Mecca surrendered without a fight, after the Meccans received a promised, which he broke the next day – but by then it was too late – that they could continue worshipping the goddesses al-Lat, al-Uzza, and Manat (Appendix The Satanic Verses) whom they considered the daughters of Allah if they became Muslims. His reputation for compassion was a result of his being uncharacteristically magnanimous with the leadership of the city and the warriors and their families, but not six men and four women who had no protectors.

Narrated Anas bin Malik:

Allah's Apostle entered Mecca in the year of its Conquest wearing an Arabian helmet on his head and when the Prophet took it off, a person came and said, "Ibn Khatal is holding the covering of the Ka'ba (taking refuge in the Ka'ba)."

The Prophet said, "Kill him."

Bukhari 29.72

Khatal was one of the Prophet's Zakat (charity) collectors who later abandon Islam and returned to Mecca. He was one of six men and four women whom the Prophet of Mercy ordered assassinated upon taking Mecca. Khatal sought the protection of the Ka'ba to no avail. Two of the four women put to death were singers in Khatal's household who years earlier as girls had song satirical songs about God's Messenger. This may, in part, explain the Prophet's pathological aversion to women singers.

The Manifest Victory

As he grew more powerful, the Prophet's increased prestige on earth and in Heaven is reflected in the nullification of revelation 46.9 about him being simply a warner, not the leader of men in Allah's Cause that he has become. Verse 46.9 also has the distinction of being the revealed truth abrogated by the greatest number of revelations.

46:9 Say: "I am not the first of the Messengers and I do not know what will be done with me or with you. I only follow what is revealed to me and I am only a manifest warner."

48:1 We have indeed given you a manifest victory,

48:2 That Allah may forgive you your former and your later sins, and complete His Blessing upon you and lead you onto a straight path;

48:3 And that Allah may give you a mighty victory.

48:4 It is He Who sent down the Serenity upon the hearts of the believers that they may increase in faith upon their faith. To Allah belongs the hosts (legions, *Moududi*) of the heavens and the earth; and Allah is All-Knowing and Wise.

48:5 That He may admit the believers, men and women, into gardens beneath which rivers flow, dwelling therein forever, and that He may remit their sins. That in Allah's Sight, is a great triumph.

> 48:6 And that He may punish the hypocrites, men and women, and the unbelievers, men and women, who think evil thoughts of Allah. Upon them is the evil turn of fortune. Allah is wrathful at them, curses them and has prepared Hell for them; and what a wretched fate!

The "manifest victory" in revelation 48:1 is the Meccans agreeing to a ten year non-aggression treaty, which the Prophet's followers, who wanted to do battle with the Meccans even if it meant defeat, considered surrender, the reason for Allah's re-assurances that it was indeed a victory.

The revelations pertaining to the "manifest victory" were communicated to His Messenger while he was riding back to Medina with his disheartened followers. It did the trick. If Allah said the Treaty of Hudaibiyah was a victory who were they to doubt God. The treaty gave the warrior Prophet the breathing space he needed to build up his forces and make alliances which would allow him to surround and conquer Mecca two years into a ten-year non-aggression pact. The Prophet could, on Allah's authority, break any treaty at his discretion if he suspected treachery.

> 8:58 And should you fear treachery from any people, throw back their treaty to them in like manner. Allah does not like the treacherous.

In January 630, on the pretence that the Meccans have been supplying arms to the Banu Bakr, a tribe allied with the Meccans which has been fighting a tribe allied with the Muslims, the Banu Khuzah, (the Meccans deny this and offer to compensate the Muslims, to no avail, for any damage the Banu Bakr may have caused), the Prophet, at the head of an army numbering at least ten thousand, marched on Mecca which is now surrounded by tribes who have converted to Islam or are allies of the Muslims.

The "mighty victory" of revelation 48:3 may not have been the bloodless surrender of Mecca, but the one-sided bloody victory over the Jewish farmers of Khaibar whose settlement the Prophet attacked and conquered in the interim (Appendix Khaibar).

One Abrogating Many

Myth of the Month of Revelations

Both the Koran and the hadiths are clear on the concept; the revelations were communicated to the Prophet during a period of twenty-three years; some while he was awake, others while he was sleeping (Appendix Dreams). Allah even admits that it was delivered piecemeal.

> 17:106 It is a Qur'an which we have divided into parts that you may recite it with deliberation, and We revealed it piecemeal.

In response to unbelievers who would only believe if the Koran was sent down all at once, Allah explained why He sent it in stages.

> 25:32 The unbelievers say: "If only this Qur'an had been sent down on him all at once." That is how We wanted to strengthen your heart with it and We have revealed it in stages.
>
> 25:33 They never bring you any simile but We bring the truth and a better exposition.
>
> 25:34 Those who are mustered on their faces in Hell; those are in a worse position and are more wayward.

These unbelievers, judging from Allah trademark overreaction i.e. the face down in Hell reference, probably wanted a complete Koran as proof that His last and greatest Messenger was not making it up as he went along (Appendix Accusations of Plagiarism and Fabrication).

Yet, the idea persist that the Koran was delivered during the month of Ramadan which an abrogating revelation does nothing to dispel. Verse 2:185 is not unlike other revealed truths where the idea seems to come to God to be more specific about one of His many requirements; in this instance, when to fast and for how long.

2:183 O you who believe, fasting is prescribed for you as it was prescribed for those before you, so that you may be God-fearing;

2:184 For a fixed number of days. If any of you is sick or on a journey, then [an equal] number

2:185 The month of Ramadan is the month in which the Qur'an was revealed, providing guidance for mankind, with clear verses to guide and to distinguish right from wrong. He who witnesses that month should fast it. But if anyone is sick or on a journey,

of other days. And those who find it extremely difficult (to fast) should, as a penance, feed a poor man. He who spontaneously does more good (increases the penance) it is for his own good. To fast is better for you, if only you knew. [he ought to fast] a number of other days. Allah desires ease and does not desire hardship for you, that you may complete the total number [of fasting days]; glorify Allah for His Guidance, and that you may be thankful.

Something for the Tax Collector

Revelation 9:60 abrogates revelation 2:215 and allocates part of "the bounty" to pay those who collect the tax, to buy off enemies of Islam, to pay unbelievers who will not help the believers otherwise and on war-making to subdue those who will not submit (the part about "spending in Allah's Path") ...

2:215 They ask you (the question was put to the Messenger by a wealthy old man) what they should spend. Say: "Whatever bounty you give is for the parents, the near of kin, the orphans the needy and the wayfarer. And whatever good you do, Allah is fully cognizant of it."

51:19 And of their possessions, the beggar and the destitute had as share.

9:60 The alms are for the poor, the needy, their collectors and those whose hearts are bound together ("'those whose hearts are to be won over' A portion of Zakat Funds may also be given to win over to Islam those who might be engaged in anti-Islamic activities or to those in the camp of the unbelievers who might be brought to help the Muslims ..." *Moududi*), as well as for the freeing of slaves, [repaying] the debtors, spending in Allah's Path, and for the wayfarer. Thus Allah commands. Allah is All-Knowing, Wise.

Abrogated revelation 51:19 is part of a series of revealed truths about another aspect of Judgement Day. Make of it what you will! In any event, it is no longer valid.

> 51:12 They ask: "When is the Day of Judgement coming?"
>
> 51:13 The Day they shall be exposed to the Fire.
>
> 51:14 "Taste your ordeal; this is what you were trying to hasten (the Meccan unbelievers made fun of the Prophet by asking him to hasten the punishment)."
>
> 51:15 The God-fearing shall be amidst gardens and springs;
>
> 51:16 Availing themselves of what their Lord has given them. Before that time, they were beneficent.
>
> 51:17 They used to sleep but a short watch of the night;

51:18 And at daybreak, they used to ask for forgiveness,

51:19 And of their possessions, the beggar and the destitute had as share.

More Brides for Believers

For most men one of the more seductive features of Islam is the right to be married to four females simultaneously.

With a ratio of approximately 101 pubescent boys to 100 pubescent girls – a ratio which would have been even higher in favour of males during the Prophet's time – where were the believers expected to find those extra wives without leaving other deserving men without? This problem could be why Allah made the Women of the Book, abrogator 5:5, the wives and daughters of Christians and Jews halal i.e. okay to marry. There was of course no quid pro quo. Revealed truth 2:221 about not marrying polytheists may have been abrogated in the process because it was pointless since believers in more than one god or goddesses are to be put to death on the spot if they do not convert on demand. Why revelation 6:121 about halal meat in the abrogated column, I have no clue, but I suspect many will find it an interesting juxtaposition.

2:221 Do not marry unbelieving women (polytheists) until they believe. A believing slave-girl is certainly better than an unbelieving woman, even if the latter pleases you. And do not give your women (believing women) in marriage to polytheists until they believe. A believing slave is certainly better than a polytheist even if the latter pleases you. Those (the polytheists) call to the Fire and Allah calls to Paradise and Forgiveness by His Leave; and He makes clear His Revelations to mankind so that they may be mindful.

6:121 And do not eat from that over which the Name of Allah has not been mentioned; it is indeed sinful. The devils shall insinuate to their followers to dispute with you; but if you obey them, then you will surely be polytheists.

5:5 This day the good things have been made lawful to you; the food of the People of the Book is lawful to you, and your food is lawful to them; and so are the believing women who are chaste, and the chaste women of those who were given the Book before you, provided you give them their dowries and take them in marriage, not in fornication or as mistresses. If any one denies the faith, his work shall be of no avail to him, and in the Hereafter he will rank with the losers.

Of all the gods I have studied, none is as strategic a long-term thinker as Allah. Not only did the four wives per believer bring men flocking to His Messenger's banner, but by making the wives and daughters of

People of the Book eligible for matrimony, He increased the progeny of believers at the expense of the unbelievers. In addition, a child born in a Muslim household is a Muslim for life, to even think of leaving the Perfect Religion is a death sentence (Appendix Apostates Koran, Apostates Hadiths).

The late Muammar Gaddafi boasted that the Muslim birthrate (and death for those who would abandon Islam, I would add), will, without the need for swords or guns or military conquests, in a matter of a few decades overwhelm the European kuffars (pejorative term for non-Muslims). The fact that second and especially third-generation immigrants' birthrates are much closer to the national norm may moderate his prediction.

First, Kill All the Unbelievers

A Christian reading abrogating revelation 2:286 will be reminded of the Lord's Prayer; that is, until they get to the last sentence.

2:284 To Allah belongs whatever in the heavens and on earth. And whether you reveal or conceal what is in your hearts, Allah will call you to account for it. He will then forgive whom He wills, and punish whom He wills. He is Able to do everything.

2:285 The Messenger (Muhammad) believes in what has been revealed to him by his Lord, and so do the believers too. All believe in Allah, His Angels, His Books and His Messengers. We make no distinction between any of His Messengers. And they (the believers) say: "We hear and obey. Grant us Your Forgiveness, our Lord. And to you is our return."

2:286 Allah does not charge any soul beyond its capacity. It gets [rewarded for] what [good] it has earned, and is called to account for what [evil] it has committed. Lord, forgive us if we have forgotten or erred. Lord, do not lay on us a burden like that You laid on those before us, and do not burden us with what we cannot bear. Pardon us, forgive us and have mercy on us. You are our Protector. Give us victory over the unbelieving people.

Like all of Allah's seemingly universal declarations, there is a catch. Those who do not believe in the Koran can do all the good they can, and live an exemplary life, it won't matter a whit.

22:50 Those who believe and do the righteous deeds will receive forgiveness and a bountiful provision,

22:51 But who strive against our Revelations defying Us – those are the people of Hell.

Hell Is for Those Who Love Life

Just in case you didn't get what Allah meant by "in the Hereafter, he will have no share", revelation 42:20; it means you're going to Hell.

3:145 It is not given to any soul to die, except with Allah's Leave, at a fixed time. He who desires the reward of this world, We will give him [part] of it, and he who desires the reward of the life to come, We will give him [part] of it; and We shall reward the thankful.

42:20 He who wishes the tillage of the Hereafter, We will increase his tillage, and he who wishes the tillage of the present life, We will give him thereof; but in the Hereafter, he will have no share.

17:18 He who desires the transitory life, We hasten to him and to whomsoever We desire whatever We please. Later We consign him to Hell in which he will burn despised and rejected.

The Koran does mention houses and palaces will be made available depending on your rank in heaven (Appendix Heaven - The Nuts and Bolts) but not necessarily cultivatable land, unless tillage is again used as a metaphor for women you can have your way with.

> 2:223 Your women are a tillage for you. So get to your tillage whenever you like. Do good for yourselves, fear Allah and know that you shall meet Him. And give good news to the believers.

The Bedouins Learn Their Lesson

Early on, the Bedouins joined Allah's Cause strictly for the plunder. This made them unreliable allies. For example, after the successful defence of Medina, the Prophet decided to attempt a pilgrimage to Mecca with only lightly-armed volunteers, which the Meccans could have easily annihilated if they were so inclined. With no promise of plunder, the Bedouins refused to accompany God's Messenger, making up transparent excuses which Allah saw right through.

> 48:11 The Bedouins who stayed behind will say to you (Muhammad): "Our possessions and our families preoccupied us; so ask forgiveness for us." They say with their tongues what is not in their hearts. Say: "Who can avail you anything against Allah, if He wishes to harm you or He wishes to profit you? No, Allah is fully aware of what you do.

> 48:12 "Rather, you thought that the Messenger and the believers will never return to their families; and that was embellished in your hearts and you entertained evil thoughts and were a useless people."

The Prophet and the men who went with him did not get to do the Pilgrimage, but God's Messenger did return with a ten year non-aggression treaty with the Meccans, the Treaty of Hudaibiyah.

With Medina secured from attacks from Mecca, the Prophet and his army of holy warriors could now move against the vulnerable and prosperous Jewish settlement of Khaibar (Appendix Khaibar). This would be an easy victory with plenty for a holy warrior to plunder. Needless to say, the Bedouins were now more than eager to join the attack. God's Messenger would deny the Bedouins Khaibar, and all further plunder unless they demonstrated a genuine commitment to Allah's Cause by doing what was asked of them without hesitation.

The "desert Arabs", as Allah referred to them, had learned their lesson; and from that point on showed a devotion to Islam and God's Messenger which prompted Allah to revise his assessment of their character.

9:97 The desert Arabs are more steeped in unbelief and hypocrisy and are more likely not to know the bounds of what Allah has revealed to His Messenger. Allah is All-Knowing, Wise.

9:98 And some of the desert Arabs regard what they spend as a fine, and await the turns of fortune to go against you. May the evil turn against them. Allah is All-Hearing, All-Knowing.

9:99 And some of the desert Arabs believe in Allah and the Last Day and regard what they spend [in the way of Allah] as a means to get closer to Allah and to earn the prayers of the Messenger. Indeed, that will bring them closer [to Allah]. He will admit them into His Mercy. Allah is truly All-Forgiving, Merciful.

No More Mr. Nice Guy III

The business of civil wars tends to be a nasty business. The Arab civil war was no different, except that a god, a vengeful pitiless god took a personal interest in the conflict. This was to be expected, after all, the war was about Him. What was not expected was Allah dropping all pretences of tolerance once the war His Messenger instigated and pursued on His behalf, and which morphed into a universal jihad, started in earnest.

Before the onset of the war between the so-called pagans of Mecca and the believers of Medina, Allah expected the believers to unconditionally honour their parents. With the onset of hostilities, which would consume the entire Peninsula, Allah's intolerant nature exploded into a hatred of all generations who had not submitted to His Will. The revealed truth about honouring your parents unconditionally was replaced by another revealed truth which came with the usual strings attached.

17:23 Your Lord has decreed that you worship none but Him and to be kind to your parents. If either of them or both reach old age with you, do not say to them "Fie", nor tell them off, but say to them kind words.

17:24 And lower to them the wing of humility out of mercy and say: "Lord have mercy on them, as they took care of me when I was a child."

9:113 It is not for the Prophet and those who believe to ask for forgiveness for the polytheists even if they are near relatives, after it becomes clear to [the believers] that they are the people of the Fire.

Mercy for Adulterers and Murderers

Those who believe in Allah and only Allah including repentant murderers – but perhaps not adulterers, revelation 25:68 – will be given a shot at Paradise.

25:68 And those who do not call upon any other god than Allah, and do not kill the soul which Allah forbade, except justly; and they do not commit adultery. He who does that shall meet with retribution.

25:69 Punishment shall be doubled for him on the Day of Resurrection (Judgement Day) and he will dwell forever in it down-trodden;

25:70 Except for him who repents, believes and does the righteous deed. Those Allah will change their evil deeds into good deeds. Allah is ever All-Forgiving, Merciful.

Verse 25:68 is also abrogated by revelation 4:93 – and perhaps not if Allah is simply making it clear that premeditated murder of a believer is not a justifiable homicide, although the murderer may still be entitled to clemency and Paradise if he repents.

> 4:93 As he who kills a believer intentionally will, as punishment, be thrown into Hell, dwelling in it forever; and Allah will be angry with him, curse him and prepare for him a dreadful punishment.

You will, of course, not find a single verse about believers killing unbelievers expecting to be punished, as such murders are implicitly if not explicitly condoned unless the murdered is a Christian or a Jew who has humbly paid the right-to-live-tax i.e. the jizya.

Abrogating revelation 25:70 may allow an adulterer to repent ("Except for him who repents") and be welcomed in Paradise, but the adulteress is still out of luck.

From: **Alice visits a Mosque to learn about Judgement Day** - A play about what to expect, *Boreal Books, 2012.*

...

Imam: Allah's Mercy is for unwavering believers who have committed offenses such as stealing, killing another without just cause and so on, repented and made amends and remained steadfast in their belief in Allah's Mercy.

Alice: Am I to understand that a steadfast believer will be forgiven his transgressions if he believes he will be forgiven his transgressions?

Imam: Despairing of Allah's Mercy is not only the second greatest sin in Islam, but it is a sin against God, just like believing in other gods, and he who commits an unforgivable act, like women who commit adultery, will burn in Hell for an eternity.

Alice: Adultery is not a sin against Allah or His Messenger, so why is an adulteress not deserving of Allah's Mercy?

Imam: Because there is no way for a woman to make amends for having had sex with someone other than her husband. How would you undo that? How could she undo the dishonour that she has brought on herself, her family and her husband? It is not enough that the adulteress will roast in Hell for eternity, but steps must be taken in the here-and-now to eradicate the reminder of this dishonour and to discourage such destructive behavior.

Alice: Such as stoning the adulteress to death.

...

Not All Poets Are Perverts

Thorns in the Prophet's side until his victory over the Meccans were the poets who mocked him in verse. In victory, God's Messenger exhibited the same unforgiving pitilessness as his Mentor; he had them all killed, as he did most of his critics when the opportunity presented itself (Appendix Dead Poets).

With His vengeful Messenger having gotten rid of the troublesome wordsmiths it may have been time to turn the page, less Allah's own attempt at poetry be accused of attracting the perverts.

26:224 And as to the poets, the perverse follow them.

26:225 Do you not see that they wander aimlessly in every glen?

26:227 Except for those who believe and do the righteous deeds, mention Allah frequently, and are victorious after they were wronged. Surely, the wrongdoers

- 56 -

26:226 And that they say what they do not do.

shall know what outcome is ultimately theirs.

Evidence of a Master Copy of the Koran in Paradise

85:21 Yet, it is a glorious Qur'an,

85:22 In a Well-Preserved Tablet.

43:4 And, indeed, it is in the Mother of the Book, with Us, lofty and wise.

Revelation 42:43 abrogates two revelations from the same period, the Meccan, which are almost, and for all intents and purposes identical. These transient reveal truths are only separated by one short verse, the one in italic, meaning that the angel Gabriel could have communicated them to God's Messenger in one breath. This may be proof that there is indeed a tablet in Heaven which contains the master copy of the Koran, and once anything is carved on that tablet it cannot be erased and must be communicated as is with no alteration if the copy on earth is to be an exact replica of the copy in Heaven.

42:39 And those who, if they are oppressed, will overcome.

42:40 The reward of evil is an evil like it, but he who pardons and makes amends, his wage is with Allah. Indeed, He does not like the wrongdoers.

42:41 He who overcomes after being wronged – upon those there is no reproach

42:43 Be he who bears patiently and forgives – that is a sign of real resolve.

Revelation 42:43 is one of those sacred truths which are a tribute to sacred truths. If only there were more like it, and if only it was a sacred truth that was reveal later during the Prophet's Call, when sacred truths took on a brutal unforgiving persona.

Verse of the Sword

The Verse of the Sword abrogates more than half of the repealed revealed truths. It is without a doubt the most far-reaching revelation of the Koran. The aptly named verse is undoubtedly familiar to every jihadist and is the overriding revelation for these holy warriors.

According to the imminent Egyptian theologian Abu al-Fadl 'Abd ar-Rahman Jalal ad-Din as-Suyuti (d. 1505), "Everything in the Qur'an about forgiveness and peace is abrogated by verse 9:5."

> 9:5 Then, when the Sacred Months (these are the four months during which war was prohibited in pre-Islamic times) are over, kill the idolaters wherever you find them, take them [as captives], besiege them, and lie in wait for them at every point of observation. If they repent afterwards, perform the prayer and pay the alms then release them. Allah is truly All-Forgiving, Merciful.

You will find the Verse of the Sword in the incendiary surah Repentance – *Ultimatum* in Muhsin Khan's translation of the Koran. According to Khaleel Mohammed, assistant professor in the Department of Religious Studies at San Diego State, Khan's Saudi-approved and promoted translation is "the most widely disseminated Qur'an in Islamic bookstores and Sunni mosques throughout the English-speaking world."

Khan, born in 1927, is unequivocal about the reach of the chapter of the Koran where the Verse of the Sword is found and I quote: "God revealed *Ultimatum* in order to discard restraint and to command Muslims to fight against all the pagans as well as against the People of the Book* if they do not embrace Islam or until they pay religious taxes."

Should your inclination be not to "kill the idolaters wherever you find them" as Allah first recommends, but to take them as captives, you must still kill the pagans i.e. infidels you have corralled unless they "repent afterwards, perform the prayer and pay the alms", that is become one who submits to the Will of Allah, the most widely accepted meaning of Muslim.

----

* **Christians and Jews** – they are not to be killed or force to convert if they pay the right-to-live tax, the jizya, while acknowledging your superiority as a Muslim (next chapter Verse of the Tax).

Abrogation and Genocide

Based on Muslim chronicles of the period, and the demographic calculations done by historian K.S. Lal in his book *Growth of Muslim Population in Medieval India,* the Verse of the Sword is in all likelihood responsible for the largest known slaughter of followers of a lesser god, or gods. Dr. Lal estimates that between 1000 AD and 1500 AD the population of Hindus decreased by 80 million; meaning that for much of that period the death rate among Hindus exceeded their birthrate. If the eminent historian's estimates are even remotely accurate, this period would have witnessed the largest cold-blooded killing of an indigenous people in all written history.

A Declaration of War

The *Verse of the Sword* was received near the end of the Prophet's life when the world was very much his for the taking with Muslim armies poised to overrun much of the Middle East and North Africa. God's Messenger had already issued his ultimatum to the various rulers of the kingdoms and provinces that bordered the Peninsula, that they must convert or be invaded and converted by force. The bloodthirsty *Verse of the Sword* made that threat even more credible.

A copy of the Prophet's ultimatum has been preserved in the old Topkapi Palace in Istanbul. It is addressed to the governor of Egypt, a fellow by the name of Muqawqis. The last sentence of the ultimatum has a particularly ominous tone (italics mine).

> From Muhammad the servant and Prophet of Allah, to Muqawqis, the leader of the Coptic tribe. There is safety and security for those believers who follow the correct path. Therefore I invite you to accept Islam. If you accept it, you shall find security, save your throne, and gain twice as much reward for having introduced Islam to your followers. If you refuse this invitation, let the sin of calamity which awaits your followers be upon you. You too are People of the Book; therefore let us come to a word common between us that we worship none but Allah and shall equalise anything with him. Let us not abandon Allah and take others for lords other than him. If you do not consent to this invitation, *bear witness that we are Muslims.*

If you do not consent, we are Muslims; we do not make idle threats. Allah echoed His Messenger's warning to the People of the Book:

> 3:64 Say: 'O People of the Book, come to an equitable word between you and us, that we worship none but Allah, do not associate anything with Him and do not

set each other as lords besides Allah." If they turn their backs, say: 'Bear witness that we are Muslims.'"

The *Verse of the Sword* has a companion verse, revelation 9:111, the *Salvific Covenant* (do this for me and I will do this for you, save you, give you Paradise).

> 9:111 Allah has bought from the believers their lives and their wealth in return for Paradise; they fight in the Way of Allah, kill and get killed. That is a true promise from Him in the Torah, the Gospel and the Qur'an; and who fulfills his promise better than Allah? Rejoice then at the bargain you have made with Him; for that is the great triumph.

The *Verse of the Sword* and the *Salvific Covenant,* taken together, is the Koran's equivalent of a Declaration of War on humanity, a universal jihad until all of humankind bows down before His Eminence.

The *Verse of the Sword* does more than nullify the scattering of verses that could be interpreted as recommending mercy and compassion for unbelievers, or believers who don't believe hard enough, but consolidates for the holy warrior many of the verses about killing Allah's real and imaginary enemies in one concise paragraph.

Following are 112 revealed truths which most scholars who support the concept of abrogation agree were annulled or modified by the *Verse of the Sword;* the list, in numerical order, is from WikiIslam. It is a bit of hodgepodge. It would be highly presumptuous of me to even try to second-guess respected professional diviners of the Will of God from the Middle Ages who put the list together, so I won't. It is what it is!

2:83 When We made a covenant with the Children of Israel (saying): "You shall worship none other than Allah; show kindness to your parents, to the near of kin, to the orphans and to the poor; speak to people; perform the prayers; give the alms-tax." But, with the exception of a few, you did not abide by the covenant and you turned away.

2:139 Say: "Do you dispute with us concerning Allah when He is our Lord and your Lord? We have our works (by which we shall be judged) and you have your works (by which you shall be judged). To Him alone we are devoted.

2:190 And fight for the Cause of Allah those who fight you, but do not be aggressive. Surely Allah does not like the aggressor.

Revelation 2:190, perhaps for emphasis, is also abrogated by the verse about the right religion, the right months and fighting as a group.

> 9:36 The number of months, with Allah, is twelve months by Allah's Ordinance from the day He created the heavens and the earth. Four of these are Sacred. This is the right religion, so do not wrong yourselves during them; but fight the polytheists all together just as they fight you all together; and know that Allah is on the side of the righteous.

The Sacred Months are a holdover from the pagans, as are many of Islam's rituals, often with slight modifications; for example, no more circumambulating the Ka'ba naked. A less benign adaptation was Allah allowing killing your rivals during the sacred months, which was strictly forbidden by the pagans. He did this to justify the murder of the first unbeliever, a fellow by the name of Amr-ben-al Hadra'mi (Appendix The Murder of Amr-ben-al Hadra'mi) at the outset of the sacred time.

2:191 Kill them wherever you find them and drive them out wherever they drove you out (from Mecca). Sedition is worse than slaughter. Do not fight them at the Sacred Mosque until they fight you at it. If they fight you there kill them. Such is the reward for the unbelievers.

2:192 But if they desist, Allah is truly All-Forgiving, Merciful.

2:217 They ask you about the sacred month: "Is there fighting in it?" Say: "Fighting in it is a great sin; but to debar people from Allah's Way and to deny Him and the Sacred Mosque, and to drive its people out of it is a greater sin in Allah's Sight. Sedition is worse than murder." Nor will they cease to fight you until they make you, if they can, renounce your religion. Those of you who renounce their religion and die, while they are unbelievers, are those whose works come to grief, [both] in this world and in the Hereafter. And they are the people of the Fire, abiding in it forever.

2:256 There is no compulsion in religion; true guidance has become distinct from error. Thus he who disbelieves in the Devil and believes in Allah grasps the firmest handle that will never break. Allah is All-Hearing, All-Knowing.

3:20 So, if they dispute with you, say: "I have submitted myself to Allah and so have those who followed me"; and say also to those who have received the Book and to the unlearned (the Arab idolaters of Mecca): "Have you submitted?" If they have submitted, then they are rightly guided; but if they have turned their backs, then your duty is simply to deliver the Message. Allah perceives His servants well.

3:28 Let not the believers take the unbelievers for friends, rather than the believers. Whoever does that has nothing to do with Allah, unless you guard against them fully! Allah warns you to beware of Him (warns you of His anger); and unto Him is the ultimate return!

Revelation 3:28 is also abrogated by revelation 8:57 in which Allah replaces a decree about not associating with unbelievers with one that demands you be brutal with them for reasons He makes obvious.

> 8:57 So, if you should come upon them in the war, scatter (punish them severely) them with those behind them, that perchance they may pay heed.

4:63 Allah knows what is in the hearts of those ones; so leave them alone, admonish them and say to them effective words about themselves.

4:80 Whoever obeys the Messenger actually obeys Allah. As for those who turn away, We have not sent you to be their helpers.

4:81 They say: "Obedience"; but when they leave you, a group of them secretly plan something other than what you say. Allah writes down what they have in mind. So shun them and put your trust in Allah; Allah is the All-Sufficient Guardian.

4:84 So, fight for the cause of Allah; you are charged only of yourself. Urge the believers on that Allah may perchance restrain the unbelievers' might. Allah's might is greater, and greater is His Retribution!

4:90 Except for those who seek refuge with a people with whom you are bound by a compact, or come to you because their hearts forbid them to fight you or fight their own people. Had Allah wished, He would have made them dominate you; and then they would have certainly fought you. If, however, they leave you alone and do not fight you and offer you peace, then Allah allows you no way against them.

4:91 You shall find others who wish to be secure from you and secure from their own people; yet whenever they are called back to sedition (polytheism) they plunge into it. If these do not keep away from you, nor offer you peace, nor hold their hands back, then seize them and kill them wherever you find them. Those we have given you clear authority over them.

4:140 He has revealed to you in the Book that, should you hear the Revelations of Allah being denied or mocked, you should not sit with them until they engage in some other discussion. Otherwise, you are like them. Allah shall assemble all the hypocrites and the unbelievers in Hell;

5:2 O believers, do not violate the Rites of Allah, or the Sacred Month, or the sacrificial offerings, or the animals with garlands, or those who repair to the Sacred House seeking the bounty and pleasure of their Lord. When you are through with the rites of pilgrimage, you can go hunting. And let not the hatred of those who debar you from the Sacred Mosque prompt you to transgress. Help one another in righteousness and piety, but not in sin and aggression. Fear Allah; Allah is Severe in retribution.

5:13 And on account of them violating their covenant, We cursed them and caused their hearts to harden; they take the words (the words in the Torah) out of their context and forget part of what they were enjoined, and you do not cease to find them treacherous, except for a few of them. Yet, pardon them and forgive; Allah surely loves those who do good to others.

5:99 The duty of the Messenger is only to deliver the Message, and Allah knows what you reveal and you conceal.

6:66 And your people deny it (the Qur'an), whereas it is the truth. Say: "I am not your guardian."

6:68 And when you see those who talk scornfully about Our Revelations, turn away from them, until they engage in another discourse. And should the devil cause you to forget, do not sit down with the evil-doing-people.

6:70 And leave those who take their religion for sport and who are deluded by the life of this world, and remind by it (the Qur'an), lest any soul should perish of what it has earned (on account of the person's deeds). Apart from Allah, it has no protector or intercessor; and if it offers any ransom, it will not be accepted from it. Such are those who are turned over [to be punished] on account of what they have earned. They will have a drink of boiling water and a very painful punishment, because they disbelieved.

6:91 They do not show proper regard for Allah's Greatness when they say: "Allah has not revealed anything to a mortal." Say: "Who revealed the Book which was brought by Moses as a light and guidance to mankind? You put it in scrolls which you reveal, while you conceal much. And [now] you are taught (in the Koran) what neither you nor your fathers knew." Say: "Allah [revealed it]. Then leave them to revel in their nonsense."

6:104 Clear proofs have come to you from your Lord. Thus he who perceives, perceives for his own advantage, and he who is blind, that is to his lost; and I am not your Keeper.

6:106 Follow what has been revealed to you from your Lord; for there is no god but He; and turn away from the polytheists.

6:107 Had Allah pleased, they would not have associated [other gods]; and We have not made you their keeper, and you are not their guardian.

6:108 Do not curse (Muhammad) those [deities] whom they call upon besides Allah, lest they wrongfully curse Allah without knowledge. Thus We have made the deeds of every nation seem fair to them; then unto their Lord is their return, and He will tell them what they were doing.

6:112 Likewise, We have assigned to every Prophet an enemy, the devils of men and jinn, revealing one to the other tawdry speech in order to deceive; but had your Lord willed, they would not have done it. So leave them to what they invent;

6:137 And likewise, their associate-gods have insinuated to them the killing of their children, so as to destroy them and confound them in their religion. Had Allah pleased they would not have done it. So leave them (Muhammad) to their fabrications.

6:159 Surely, you are not in any way part of those who have differentiated between parts of their religion and split into sects. Their fate is in Allah's Hands. He will inform them if what they have done.

7:183 And I will grant them respite. Surely My Scheme is very effective.

7:199 Hold to forgiveness, enjoin the good and turn away from the ignorant.

8:61 And if they incline to peace, incline to it too, and put your trust in a Allah. He is truly the Hearer, the Knower. * 9:29

8:72 Those who have believed and emigrated and struggled with their wealth and their lives in the part of Allah, and those who gave refuge and support – those are friends of one another; but those who have believed, yet did not emigrate, you will not be responsible for their protection until they emigrate. Should they seek your support for religion's sake, you ought to support them, but not against a people with whom you have a compact. Allah is Fully Aware of what you do.

8:73 As to the unbelievers, they are friends of one another. If you do not do this (subdue the unbelievers), there will be great sedition and corruption in the land.

9:2 Travel, then, in the land freely for four months, and know that you will never able to thwart Allah, and that Allah shall disgrace the unbelievers.

9:7 How can the idolaters have a compact with Allah and His Messenger, except for those you made a compact (a formal treaty) with at the Sacred Mosque? So long as these honour their obligations to you, honour yours to them. Allah loves the righteous.

10:41 If they deny what you say, then say (O Muhammad): "What I do is mine, and what you do is yours. You are quit of what I do, and I am quit of what you do."

10:99 Had your Lord willed, everybody on earth would have believed. Will you then compel people to become believers?

10:108 Say: "O people, the truth has come to you from your Lord; whoever is well-guided is well-guided only to his own advantage, and whoever goes astray goes astray only to his disadvantage, and I am not a guardian over you."

11:12 Perhaps you are passing over (not reciting) a part of what is revealed to you, and your heart is distressed lest they should say: "If only a treasure was sent down upon him or an angel accompanied him!" You are only a warner, and Allah is in charge of everything.

11:121 "And say to the unbelievers: "Continue with what you are doing, and We shall continue with ours.

11:122 And wait; we too are waiting."

13:40 And whether We show you part of what We promised them or cause you to die, your duty is to deliver the Message and it is for Us to do the reckoning.

15:3 Leave them to eat, enjoy themselves and let [false] hopes beguile them; for they will soon know.

15:85 We have not created the heavens and the earth and what lies between them save in truth; and the Hour (Judgement Day) is surely coming. So forgive them (your detractors) magnanimously.

15:88 Do not strain your gaze towards what We gave certain groups of them to enjoy, and do not grieve for them, and lower your wing (be modest) to the believers.

15:89 And say: "I am truly the plain warner."

15:94 So proclaim what you are commanded and turn away from the polytheists.

16:82 Then, if they turn away, your duty (Muhammad) is to deliver the clear Message.

16:125 Call to the Way of Your Lord with wisdom and mild exhortation, and argue with them in the best manner. Your Lord surely knows those who stray from His Path, and He knows well those who are rightly guided.

16:127 Be patient; yet your patience is only through Allah. Do not grieve for them (the unbelievers), and do not be distressed on account of what they devise.

17:54 Your Lord knows you best. If He pleases, He will have mercy on you, and if He pleases He will torture you. We have not sent you (Muhammad) to be their guardian.

19:39 And warn them of the Day of sorrow, when the issue is decided, while they are heedless and do not believe.

19:75 Say (O Muhammad): "Whoever is in error, let the Compassionate prolong his term; so that when they are threatened with, whether it be the punishment or the Hour, they will know who is worse in position and weaker in supporters."

19:84 So do not hasten (O Muhammad) [their punishment] We are indeed counting for them the days.

20:130 So bear (Muhammad) patiently what they say, and celebrate the praise of your Lord before the rising of the sun and before its setting; and glorify him during the hours of the night and at the two ends of the day, that you may be well-pleased.

20:135 Say: "Everybody is waiting, so wait; and then you will know who are the people of the Straight Path and who are the well-guided."

22:68 And if they dispute with you, say: "Allah knows best what you are doing."

23:54 So, leave them in their error for a while.

24:54 Say: "Obey Allah and obey the Messenger; but if you turn away, then upon him (the Prophet) rests what he was charged with, and upon you what you were charged with. However, if you obey him, you will be well-guided. It is only incumbent on the Messenger to deliver the manifest message."

25:63 And the servants of the Compassionate who walk in the land gently and, if the ignorant address them, they say: "Peace."

27:92 And to recite the Qur'an. He who is well-guided is only well-guided to his own advantage, and to him who goes astray, say: "I am only one of the warners."

28:55 And when they hear idle talk, they turn away from it and say: "We have our works and you have your works. Peace be upon you; we do not desire the company of the ignorant."

29:50 They said: "If only signs from his Lord were sent down on him (Muhammad)." Say: "Signs are only with Allah, and I am only a manifest warner."

30:60 Be patient then, for Allah's Promise is true; and do not be disheartened by those who lack the certitude of faith.

31:23 Whoever disbelieves, let not his disbelief sadden you. Unto us is their return and then We will tell them what they did. Allah knows well the secret of the breasts.

32:30 So turn away from them and wait; they too shall be waiting.

33:48 And do not obey the unbelievers and the hypocrites, overlook their injury, and trust in Allah. For Allah suffices as Guardian.

34:25 Say: "You will not be questioned about our misdeeds and we will not be questioned about what you do."

35:23 You are only a warner.

36:76 Do not let their words cause you grief; We know what they reveal and what they conceal.

37:174 So, turn away (O Muhammad) from them for a while.

37:175 And look at them; they shall soon be able to see (their defeat and your victory with their own eyes, Moududi).

37:178 And turn away from them a while.

37:179 And look, for they shall be able to see.

38:70 "It is only revealed to me that I am a manifest warner."

38:88 "And you will learn its message after a while."

39:3 Sincere religion belongs to Allah. Those who took other protectors, apart from Him, say: "We only worship them so as to bring us closer to Allah in rank". Allah surely judges between them with respect with what they differ upon. Allah surely does not guide him who is a thankless liar.

39:14 Say (O Muhammad): "Allah alone I worship professing to Him my religion sincerely.

39:15 "Worship, then, what you wish, apart from Him." Say: "Indeed, those who have lost themselves and their families on the Day of Resurrection are the real losers. That is truly the manifest lost."

39:36 Does not Allah suffice His servant? Yet they frightened you with those apart from Him (that is, idols). Whomever Allah leads astray will have no other guide.

39:39 Say: "My people, act according to your ability. I am acting; then you will know.

39:40 "Whoever is visited by punishment will be degraded by it and a lasting punishment will befall him."

39:41 We have sent the Book upon you for all mankind in truth. He who is well-guided is guided to his own gain, and he who goes astray, will go astray to his loss. You are not their overseer.

39:46 Say: "O Allah, Creator of the heavens and the earth, Knower of the Unseen and the Seen, you shall judge between your servants regarding that whereon they used to differ."

40:12 That is because if Allah is called upon alone, you disbelieve; but if others are associated with Him, you believe. Judgement is Allah's the All-High, the All-Great.

40:55 So stand fast; Allah's Promise is true. Seek the forgiveness of your sin and proclaim the praise of your Lord evenings and mornings.

40:77 So, bear up patiently; Allah's Promise is true. We will either show you (Muhammad), what We are promising them, or We will call you unto Us. Then unto us they will be brought back.

41:34 The fair and evil deeds are not equal. Respond with that which is fairer, so that he against whom you have a grudge shall be like an intimate friend.

42:6 Those who have taken other protectors, apart from Him, Allah oversees them and you are not their guardian.

42:15 Therefore, summon and be upright as you were commanded, and do not follow their fancies, but say: "I believe in whatever Book Allah has sent down. I have been commanded to judge justly between you. Allah is our Lord and your Lord; we have our deeds and you have your deeds. There is no dispute between us and you; Allah will gather us together and unto Him is our ultimate return."

42:48 Should they turn away, We have not sent you as guardian to watch over them; incumbent on you is delivering the Message only. Indeed, when We make man taste a mercy from Us, he rejoices in it, but when they are afflicted with a misfortune, on account of what their hands had previously perpetrated, then man is truly thankless.

43:83 So leave them to romp and frolic till they encounter their Day (Judgement Day) which they have been promised.

43:89 So turn away from them, and say: "Peace." For they will certainly come to know.

44:59 So wait and watch; they are waiting and watching.

45:14 Tell the believers to forgive those who do not hope for Allah's Days (evil days from Allah, Moududi, calamities mostly, Fakhry), that He may reward a people for what they used to earn.

46:35 So bear patiently, as the Constant Messengers (Noah, Abraham, Moses and Jesus) bore up, and do not seek to hasten it (the punishment) for them. On that Day they shall see what they were promised, as if they had not lingered except for a single hour of the day. This is a proclamation. Shall any but the sinful people be destroyed?

47:4 So when you meet the unbelievers, strike their necks till you have bloodied them then fasten the shackles. Thereupon, release them freely or for a ransom till the war is over. So be it. Yet had Allah wished, He would have taken vengeance upon them, but he wanted to test you by one another. Those who die in the Cause of Allah, He will not render their works perverse.

50:39 Bear up with what they say and proclaim the Praise of your Lord before sunrise and before sunset.

50:45 We know better what they say and you are not a tyrant terrorizing them. So, remind, by the Qur'an, him who fears My Warning.

52:31 Say: "Await, I am indeed with you awaiting."

52:45 Leave them, then, till they encounter the Day on which they will be thunderstruck;

52:48 Bear with your Lord's Judgement, for you are in Our Thoughts; and proclaim the Praise of Your Lord when you arise;

53:29 So turn away from him who has given up Our Reminder (the Qur'an) and only desire the present life.

54:6 Turn away from them. On the Day the caller shall call out an abominable thing;

60:11 If any of your wives desert you to the unbelievers, and you decide to penalize them, then give those [husbands] whose wives have gone away the like of what they have spent (the dowry), and fear Allah in whom you believe.

68:44 So, leave Me alone with those who disbelieve this discourse. We shall draw them out whence they do not know.

68:48 Bear up with your Lord's Judgement, then, and do not be like the Man in the Whale (Jonah), when he called out fully distressed.

70:5 Bear up patiently then (Muhammad).

70:42 So leave them to romp and play till they meet their Day, which they have been promised.

73:10 And bear up with what they say, and forsake them graciously.

73:11 And let Me deal with those who deny and live in luxury; and give them a little respite.

74:11 Leave Me with him (al-Walid Ibn al-Mughirah) whom I created alone,

76:8 And they give food, despite their love of it, to the destitute, the orphans and the captive.

76:24 So bear up with your Lord's Judgement and do not obey (Muhammad) any sinful or thankless one of them.

76:29 This indeed is a reminder; so he who wishes will follow, unto His Lord, a path.

86:17 So (Muhammad), give the unbelievers some respite. Respite them slowly.

88:21 So, exhort, you (Muhammad) are a mere exhorter;

88:22 You are not supposed to dominate (compel, Moududi) them;

88:23 Except for him who turns away and disbelieves;

95:8 Is not Allah the Best of Judges?

109:6 "You have your religion and I have mine."

Verse of the Tax

After the Verse of the Sword, the Verse of the Tax impacts the most revelations, although the Verse of the Sword remains the master abrogator, and by a substantial margin. In the Verse of the Tax, Allah commands that the People of the Book – Christians, Jews and an obscure sect, but not to Allah, the Sabians – pay the jizya, a yearly poll-tax (a tax on people as opposed to property).

> 9:29 Fight those among the People of the Book who do not believe in Allah and the Last Day, do not forbid what Allah and His Messenger have forbidden and do not profess the true religion, till they pay the poll-tax out of hand and submissively.

This concession to a modicum of mercy, if you paid for it, is not available to infidels i.e. those who do not worship the One God.

God's Messenger first tried to impose the jizya after the *Battle of Badr*, the first real battle in the Arab Civil War between the believers and unbelievers which started it all. The Jews ridiculed his proposal saying that Allah could not be so poor as to require their money.

The jizya became a fact of life for the People of the Book after the conquest of the Jewish settlement of Khaibar (Appendix Khaibar).

The Verse of the Tax abrogates some of the revealed truths modified or invalidated by the Verse of the Sword (revelations 5:13, 6:70, 8:61, 42:15) and are not repeated here. The first revelation, in numerical order, abrogated by the Verse of the Tax is another of those revealed truths where Allah admits He needs time to come up with a more permanent solution to a perceived problem, and that He will get back to you.

> 2:109 Many of the people of the Book (Jews and Christians) wish, out of envy, to turn you back into unbelievers after the Truth has become manifest to them. But pardon and overlook, until Allah makes known His Will. Surely Allah has the power over all things.

Verse 2:109 was abrogated, along with revelations 3:111 and 3:186 (the part about Christian and Jews), once Allah came up with His targeted people tax as part of His solution to difficulties posed by the People of the Book doing a little proselytizing of their own.

3:111 They will only cause you a little harm; and if they fight you, they will turn their backs on you (run away), and will have no support.

3:186 You shall be tried in your possessions and yourselves, and shall hear from those who received the Book before you (the Jews and Christians) and from the idolaters, a lot of abuse; but if you forebear and guard against evil, that indeed is a mark of great determination.

Probably the most significant and the most lamented (by the people targeted by Allah's people tax) invalidated revealed truth, is verse 29:46 where Allah displays a rare tolerance of other faiths who worship a variation of His Eminence. You guessed it, it is a revealed truth from the more accommodating Meccan period. Pity!

29:46 Do not dispute with the people of the Book save in the fairest way; except for those of them who are evildoers. And say: "We believe in what has been sent down to us and what has been sent down to you. Our God and your God are one and to Him we are submissive."

Afterword

Putting Words in God's Mouth

How is it possible for an omniscient i.e. al-knowing, all-seeing god to be confused about the number of late arrivals He will allow into His Paradise? It is possible that it is the scholars who got it wrong, not Allah. For example, the revealed truth which precedes revelation 56:14 is abrogated by a verse which would be identical if it was not for the word "goodly" which was added by scholars.

| 56:13 A throng of the ancients. | 56:39 A (goodly) throng of the ancients, |

Revealed truth 56:40 which abrogates an almost identical revealed truth, revelation 56:14, could have been inspiration for the title *Your Guide to Abrogations* for it neatly encapsulate what the book is all about in Allah revising His estimate of the number of "latecomers" He will allow into Paradise, from a few i.e. "a small band" to a multitude i.e. "a throng".

| 56:14 And a small band of the latecomers*. | 56:40 And a throng of the latecomers. |

It may be that Allah was not as much into rephrasing what he revealed, as were the scholars who tried to bring order to what British historian Thomas Carlyle described as "a confused, jumble, crude, incondite, endless iteration..." and Edward Gibbon "as toilsome a reading as I ever undertook; a wearisome confused jumble."

Having spent only slightly more than a decade reading and re-reading and writing about the Koran, unlike those who have spent a lifetime studying Islamic scriptures in an attempt to explain what, to the unschooled in revealed truths appears to so much nonsense, I must admit I may not be qualified to answer, even if the answer for the layperson may be obvious.

----

* The revelation about the latecomers is part of a group of revealed truths about the variety and abundance of sex god-fearing men can expect in Paradise.

> 56:35 We have formed them originally;
>
> 56:36 And made them pure virgins,
>
> 56:37 Tender and unageing,
>
> 56:38 For the Companions of the Right,

56:39 A throng of the ancients,

56:40 And a throng of the latecomers.

APPENDICES

Abraham at Mecca

Excerpt from:
Shared Prophets, Boreal Books

2:125 And [remember] when We made the House (the Ka`ba) a place of residence for mankind and a haven [saying]: "Make of Abraham's maqam [stand] a place for prayer." We enjoined Abraham and Isma`il [saying]: "Purify My House for those who circle it, for those who retreat there for meditation, and for those who kneel and prostrate themselves (perform the prayers)."

2:126 And when Abraham said: "My Lord make this a secure city and feed with fruits those of its inhabitants who believe in Allah and the Last Day." Allah (having accepted Abraham's prayer) said: "As for those who disbelieve, I shall provide for them for a while (in this life), and then subject them to the scourge of the Fire, and what an abominable fate!"

If the Islamic tradition that Adam set up the original altar at Mecca using the stone he brought with him from Paradise has any connection with reality, then people were already circling the Ka`ba when Abraham and Isma'il showed up. Where the Tradition falls down a bit, is if we give "raised the foundations" in revelation 2:127 its ordinary, everyday meaning.

2:127 And while Abraham and Isma`il raised the foundations of the House, [they prayed]: "Our Lord, accept [this] from us. Surely you are the All-Hearing, the Omniscient."

It is while labouring at laying (or rebuilding) the foundations of the Ka`ba that Abraham asked Allah to send the Koran, of whose existence in heaven he was obviously aware.

2:128 "Our Lord, cause us to submit to You, and make of our posterity a nation that submits to You. Show us our sacred rites, and pardon us. You are, indeed, the Pardoner, the Merciful."

2:129 "Our Lord, send them a Messenger from among themselves (*Arabs*) who will recite to them Your Revelations, to teach them the Book (the Koran) and the wisdom, and to purify them. You are truly the Mighty, the Wise."

Abraham is the chosen one, an example of one who does what he is told, and this will be Abraham's legacy.

> 2:130 And who would forsake the religion of Abraham except one who makes a fool of himself? We have chosen him in this world and in the Hereafter; he shall be one of the righteous.

> 2:131 When His Lord told him (Abraham): "Submit", he said: "I have submitted to the Lord of the Worlds."

> 2:132 And Abraham bequeathed that to his sons, and so did Jacob saying: "O my sons, Allah has chosen the religion for you; so do not die except as submitting people."

Eve, and later Adam, as mentioned in *Adam - Paradise Lost* were the first to disturb the sands of the future city at the center of the universe. In surah 14, *Abraham (Abrâhim)*, Allah reveals more about Abraham at Mecca. These revelations may have to do with a second visit, the clue being the mention of many sons in revelation 14:35.

> 14:35 And [remember] when Abraham said: "Lord, make this town secure, and keep me and my sons from worshipping the idols.

> 14:36 "Lord, they have led (the idols) many people astray; therefore he who follows me, shall belong to me, and he who disobeys me, surely You are All-Forgiving, Merciful.

> 14:37 "Our Lord, I have settled some of my offspring in a valley which has no tillage, by Your Sacred House, so that, Lord, they may perform the prayer. Make, then, the hearts of some people incline towards them, and provide them with some fruits, that perchance they might give thanks.

> 14:38 "Our Lord, You know what we conceal and what we reveal, and nothing on earth or in heaven is concealed from Allah.

> 14:39 "Praise be to Allah, who has given me, in old age, Isma`il and Isaac. Surely my Lord is the Hearer of Prayer.

> 14:40 "Lord, make and my posterity keep up the prayers; and, our Lord, accept my supplication.

> 14:41 "Our Lord, forgive me, my parents and the believers, on the Day when the reckoning shall come to pass."

Accusations of Plagiarism and Fabrication

Excerpt from:
From Merchant to Messenger, Boreal Books

Allah acknowledges that many of His Messenger's contemporaries accused the Prophet of plagiarism.

> 25:5 And they say: "Legends of the ancients which he solicited their writing down. Hence they are dictated to him morning and evening."

> 25:6 Say: "He Who knows the secret in the heavens in the earth has sent it down; He is indeed All-Forgiving, Merciful."

An example using a famous saying of Jesus: "It will be easier for a camel to pass through the eye of a needle than for a rich man to enter the Kingdom of Heaven (Mathew 16:23)."

> 7:40 Indeed, those who have denied Our Revelations and rejected them arrogantly – the gates of heaven shall not be opened for them and they shall not enter Paradise until the camel passes through the eye of the needle. Thus we punish the wicked sinners.

If it was plagiarism, would Allah have even mentioned it?

> 6:25 And some of them listen to you, but We have cast veils over their hearts, lest they should understand it (the Qur'an) and a deafness in their ears. And even where they see every sign, they will not believe in it; so that when they come to dispute with you, the unbelievers will say: "This is nothing but fables of the ancients."

> 6:26 And they forbid others from [following] him (the Prophet), and they keep away from him, but they only destroy themselves, without perceiving it.

The Prophet's purported illiteracy, for a successful merchant, would have been a serious handicap even during the Dark Ages. During this period, just like the time before the invention of writing, facts and fiction effortless mixed in stories told and re-told, with countless variations, and passed down from generation to generation in what is known as oral tradition.

The Koran is a product of these oral traditions. God's Messenger could not be accused of plagiarism for repeating "Fables of the ancients", if that is what he did, since this was done all the time.

> 8:31 And when Our Revelations are recited to them, they say: "We have heard. Had we wished, we would have uttered the like of this; this is nothing but fables of the ancients."

> 16:24 And if it is said to them: "What has your Lord revealed?" they say: "Fables of the ancients."

What about accusations that the Koran is a fabrication?

> 25:4 The unbelievers say: "This (the Qur'an) is nothing but deceit, which he (Muhammad) has invented and was assisted therein by other people (the Jews)." They have simply come up with wrongdoing and falsehood.

Some of the accusations of fabrication may have been the result of Allah changing his mind. The pre-Islamic Arabs were a practical no-nonsense people. The logic of an omniscient god who knows everything, including the future, and is never wrong, changing His mind was simply inconceivable. It was profoundly illogical! They simply did not buy Allah's argument in revelation 2:106 that abrogating i.e. replacing one revelation with another was His prerogative. A stupefying concept in and of itself!

> 2:106 Whichever verse We abrogate or cause to be forgotten, We bring instead a better or similar one. Do you not know that Allah has the power over all things?

It did not matter that Allah revealed that He knows what He is doing when He replaces "a verse with another", and you have the angel Gabriel's word on it – "the Holy Spirit" in revelation 16:102.

> 16:101 And if We replace a verse by another – and Allah knows best what He reveals – they say: "You are only a forger." Surely, most of them do not know.

> 16:102 Say: "The Holy Spirit has brought it down from your Lord in truth, in order to reassure the believers, and as a guidance and good news to those who submit.

Furthermore, it's not that His Messenger got a revelation wrong because he heard it in a foreign language (the person alluded to here is undoubtedly a Jew) that an earlier revelation was changed, as Allah only transmits His revelations in Arabic.

> 16:103 And We surely know that they say: "Surely a mortal teaches him." The tongue of him to whom they allude is foreign, whereas this is a clear Arabic tongue.

26:192 And this (the Qur'an) is the revelation of the Lord of the Worlds;

26:193 Brought down by the Faithful Spirit (Gabriel),

26:194 Upon your heart (O Muhammad), so that you might be one of the warners;

26:195 In manifest Arabic tongue.

Research into the origins of the Koran, such as that conducted in Germany by Christoph Luxenberg (pseudonym), have revealed a great number of words in Aramaic and/or Syriac which would indicate that many verses may have had a Christian or Jewish origin. Allah may be indirectly recognizing this fact in the next two revelations where He acknowledges the contribution of the Torah to the Koran and that of Jewish scholars.

26:196 And, it is, indeed, in the Scriptures of the ancients.

26:197 Is it not a sign for them that the scholars of the Children of Israel recognized it?

Allah cannot be bothered with leading those who will not be led. This is His trademark explanation when words delivered on his behalf by His Messenger fail to convince people to follow the Guide, both literally and figuratively – the revelations (the Koran) and the bringer of the revelations (the Prophet Muhammad). And for not following the Guide, the pervasive promise of a painful punishment.

16:104 Those who do not believe in Allah's Revelations shall not be guided by Allah, and a very painful punishment awaits them.

If you say it often enough that those who deny the Revelations as being God's Truth are liars, and the Koran says it often enough, the disparagement will eventually be accepted as the truth.

16:105 It is those who do not believe in Allah's revelations that fabricate falsehood. It is they who lie.

If the Koran is a fabrication, it is a pretty good fabrication, perhaps only a fabrication that a god could produce. Allah challenged anyone to produce a single chapter that is as good as one found in the Koran.

10:38 Or do they say: "He (the Prophet) has forged it." Say [O Muhammad]: "Come up, then, with a single Surah like it, and call upon whomever you can, apart from Allah, if you are truthful."

Maybe someone did, and Allah raised the ante.

> 11:13 Or will they say: "He has forged it (the Qur'an)." Say: "Come up then with ten forged surahs like it, and call upon whomever you can, apart from Allah, if you are truthful."

> 11:14 But if they do not answer you, then know that it (the Qur'an) was revealed with Allah's knowledge and that there is no god but He. Will you then submit?

What if jinn and men got together to produce a Koran?

> 17:88 Say [O Muhammad]: "Were men and jinn to band together in order to come up with the like of this Qur'an, they will never come up with the like of it, even if they back up one another."

Only the ingrates deny the Divine origins of the Koran.

> 17:89 We have indeed given mankind in this Qur'an every kind of example, but most people insist on being ungrateful.

Adam - Paradise Lost

Introduction

Excerpt from:
Shared Prophets, Boreal Books

In one Tradition of the Prophet, Adam, just before he was bodily thrown out of Paradise held onto a large stone which followed him down, both landing in present day Sri Lanka on a mountain appropriately named Adam's Peak. A rock depression near the summit, in Islamic traditions, is believed to be the footprint left by Adam when he landed. At 1.8 m, it is a sizeable dent that only a big man could have made.

Narrated Abu Huraira:

The Prophet said, "Allah created Adam in his complete shape and form (directly), sixty cubits (about 30 meters) in height. When He created him, He said (to him), 'Go and greet that group of angels sitting there, and listen to what they will say in reply to you, for that will be your greeting and the greeting of your offspring.'

Adam (went and) said, 'As-Salamu alaikum (Peace be upon you).'

They replied, 'AsSalamu-'Alaika wa Rahmatullah (Peace and Allah's Mercy be on you) So they increased 'Wa Rahmatullah'"

The Prophet added "So whoever will enter Paradise, will be of the shape and form of Adam. Since then the creation of Adam's (offspring) (i.e. stature of human beings is being diminished continuously) to the present time."

Bukhari 55:43

Adam dragged this rock all the way to where Eve was patiently waiting for him, where she landed, in the desert of present day Southern Arabia, and used this stone to set up an altar to Allah which would become the Ka'ba and around which grew the town of Mecca.

The story of Adam and Eve's fall from grace is told five times over, with small but significant variations in each retelling. This is not unusual as you will discover, with the story of Lot taking the gold for the most reiterations at nine. Eve is not mentioned by name in the Koran. The only female whose name Allah deigns to utter is that of Mary, the mother of the lesser Prophet Jesus, whom He presents, after Jesus himself, as the most credible denier of the Christian's claim that He has a son.

Allah's Mercy

Excerpt from:
Getting to Know Allah, Boreal Books

17:80 Say: "My Lord, make my entry a truthful one and my going out a truthful one, and grant me from you a supporting power."

17:81 And say: "The truth has come and falsehood has perished. Falsehood is ever perishing."

17:82 And We reveal of the Qur'an that which is healing and merciful to the believers, and it yields nothing but perdition for the wrongdoers.

In the Name of Allah, the Compassionate, the Merciful is also the phrase that you hear Muslims repeating over and over during their daily prayers and almost every time the name Allah is mentioned in print or during a conversation. This phrase in particular leaves a lay reader of the Koran somewhat perplexed since these are not qualities, as mentioned previously, we associate with Allah as our reading takes us further and further into the Koran and the mind of the Koranic God. You're only thirteen verses into the Koran (6,333 verses to go) and it starts, verse 2:7.

2:6 Those who have disbelieved, whether you warn them or not, they will not believe.

2:7 Allah has sealed their hearts and their hearing; their sight is dimmed and a terrible punishment awaits them.

2:8 There are some who say: "We believe in Allah and the Last Day;" but they are not real believers.

2:9 They seek to deceive Allah and the believers, but they deceive none other than themselves, though they are not aware of that.

2:10 In their hearts is a sickness; so Allah has increased their sickness. A painful punishment awaits them because of their lying.

More than six thousand verses later and Allah is still at it, talking about punishment and pain and burning people – men, women and children – in a raging fire.

If *compassionate* is defined as being aware of the suffering of an other and wishing to relieve it, and *merciful* as being unconditionally kind and forgiving then these are not the virtues we would associate with the author of the following verses about roasting a man over an open fire, with his wife, tethered like an animal, supplying the firewood that fuels the flame that is burning her husband.

THE FIBRE

111 Al-Masad

In the Name of Allah,
the Compassionate, the Merciful

111:1 Perish the hands of Abu Lahab, and may he perish too;

111:2 Neither his wealth nor what he has earned will avail him anything.

111:3 He will roast in a flaming fire,

111:4 And his wife will be a carrier of fire-wood,

111:5 She shall have a rope of fibre around her neck.

Does it matter that Abu Lahab and his wife were inveterate enemies of Islam in the early days? If the treatment reserved for Abu Lahab, an uncle of the Prophet, and his wife was an exception to the definition of mercy and compassion then perhaps the phrase most associated with Allah would not, for the non-believer, have such a hollow ring.

Roasting in Hell for an eternity is the fate Allah reserves for all who refuse to believe in Him and His Messenger; a fiery fate for all unbelievers which Allah never tires of reminding the readers of the Koran. Often when you come across the many verses where Allah brags about His mercy and compassion, He has just committed a merciless, pitiless act of grandiose proportions, or is about to.

Islamic tradition informs us that Allah showed what non-Muslims would consider compassion and mercy for an unbeliever only once. He spared the Prophet Muhammad's parents the torment of Hell after His Messenger was seen weeping over the tomb of his mother at Medina. When asked by people who were near him at the time why he was crying, he replied, it was because he had just seen his parents burning in Hell. Allah would bring both parents, Abdullah and Amina, back to life temporarily so that they could become Muslim and enter Paradise.

Allah is adamant! His Messenger's parents notwithstanding, all unbelievers – whether they are your children, your mother or your father – are to be shown no compassion or mercy.

Another Islamic tradition maintains that when God saw His Messenger praying for a beloved, recently deceased uncle who had sheltered him, protected him from his enemies, been a father to the young Muhammad, whose own father died before he was born, he was scolded by the angel Gabriel. The angel, in no uncertain terms, informed the Prophet that Allah did not want to see His Messenger praying for an unbeliever ever again – his uncle Abu-Talib* died an unbeliever. He reminded the Prophet that it was all pointless anyway, since unbelievers automatically go to Hell.

The further you get into the Koran the more you have difficulty accepting the contradiction of a god who claims to be compassionate and merciful while revelling in the pain He will cause you if you die an unbeliever. Then you remember; Islam is all about loyalty and the whole thing starts making sense ... *again.* Those who intone *In the Name of Allah, the Compassionate, the Merciful* during prayer and at other occasions are reminding their god that the price of their loyalty is the compassion and mercy he has promised to those who remain loyal and die believing in Him and Him only.

----

* **The Prophet** will intervene with Allah on Judgement Day and obtain a reduced sentence for his uncle:

Narrated Al-Abbas bin Abdul Muttalib:

That he said to the Prophet "You have not been of any avail to your uncle (Abu-Talib) (though) by Allah, he used to protect you and used to become angry on your behalf."

The Prophet said, "He is in a shallow fire, and had It not been for me, he would have been in the bottom of the (Hell) Fire."

Bukhari 58.222

Angels

Excerpt from:
1,001 Sayings and Deeds of the Prophet Muhammad, Boreal Books

Angels are everywhere in the Koran and in the hadiths. You cannot call yourself a Muslim if you do not believe in angels and everything Allah and His Messenger revealed about them. Some of what you will read here, and elsewhere about Allah's indispensable winged wonders may produce a sense of déja vu. If that should happen, chances are it will be a different narrator; a different companion recalling what God's Messenger said and did – more or less.

Allah is not a god who gets bored easily. Every day a billion or more believers pray five (Sunnis) and three (Shias) times a day and every day, Allah has the same conversion with his angels.

Narrated Abu Huraira:

Allah's Apostle said, "Allah has some angels who look for those who celebrate the Praises of Allah on the roads and paths. And when they find some people celebrating the Praises of Allah, they call each other, saying, 'Come to the object of your pursuit.'"

He added, "Then the angels encircle them with their wings up to the sky of the world."

He added. "(after those people celebrated the Praises of Allah, and the angels go back), their Lord, asks them (those angels) - though He knows better than them - 'What do My slaves say?'

The angels reply, 'They say: Subhan Allah, Allahu Akbar, and Alham-du-lillah (*Glorious is God, Allah is greater, Praise to God*)'.

Allah then says 'Did they see Me?'

The angels reply, 'No! By Allah, they didn't see You.'

Allah says, 'How it would have been if they saw Me?'

The angels reply, 'If they saw You, they would worship You more devoutly and celebrate Your Glory more deeply, and declare Your freedom from any resemblance to anything more often.'

Allah says (to the angels), 'What do they ask Me for?'

The angels reply, 'They ask You for Paradise.'

Allah says (to the angels), 'Did they see it?'

The angels say, 'No! By Allah, O Lord! They did not see it.'

Allah says, 'How it would have been if they saw it?'

The angels say, 'If they saw it, they would have greater covetousness for it and would seek It with greater zeal and would have greater desire for it.'

Allah says, 'From what do they seek refuge?'

The angels reply, 'They seek refuge from the (Hell) Fire.'

Allah says, 'Did they see it?'

The angels say, 'No By Allah, O Lord! They did not see it.'

Allah says, 'How it would have been if they saw it?'

The angels say, 'If they saw it they would flee from it with the extreme fleeing and would have extreme fear from it.'

Then Allah says, 'I make you witnesses that I have forgiven them.'"

Allah's Apostle added, "One of the angels would say, 'There was so-and-so amongst them, and he was not one of them, but he had just come for some need.' Allah would say, 'These are those people whose companions will not be reduced to misery.'"

Bukhari 75.417

Angels don't like those who don't spend to further Allah's plans for world domination.

Narrated Abu Huraira:

The Prophet said, "Every day two angels come down from Heaven and one of them says, 'O Allah! Compensate every person who spends in Your Cause,' and the other (angel) says, 'O Allah! Destroy every miser.'"

Bukhari 24.522

A lot of praying going on, of which Allah will be kept diligently informed by his angels.

Narrated Abu Huraira:

Allah's Apostle said, "(A group of) angels stay with you at night and (another group of) angels by daytime, and both groups gather at the time of the Asr and Fajr prayers. Then those angels who have stayed with you overnight, ascend (to Heaven) and Allah asks them (about you) - and He knows everything about you. 'In what state did you leave My slaves?' The angels reply, 'When we left them, they were praying, and when we reached them they were praying.'"

Bukhari 93.525

Try to avoid farting while praying if you want Allah to accept your prayer and the angels to keep interceding with Allah on your behalf.

Narrated Abu Huraira:

The Prophet said, "Allah does not accept prayer of anyone of you if he does hadath (passes wind) till he performs the ablution (anew)."

Bukhari 86.86

Narrated Abu Huraira:

Allah's Apostle said, "The angels keep on asking Allah's forgiveness for anyone of you, as long as he is at his Musalla (praying place) and he does not pass wind (Hadath). They say, 'O Allah! Forgive him, O Allah! be Merciful to him.'"

Bukhari 8.436

Say "Amin" at just the right time, and it will be as if you died in Allah's Cause.

Narrated Abu Huraira:

The Prophet said, "When the Imam says 'Amin', then you should all say 'Amin', for the angels say 'Amin' at that time, and he whose 'Amin' coincides with the 'Amin' of the angels, all his past sins will be forgiven."

Bukhari 75.411

It is an angel who informs Allah of a fetus' progress, and takes down Allah instructions as to what the future holds for the growing embryo.

Narrated Anas bin Malik:

The Prophet said, "Allah puts an angel in charge of the uterus and the angel says, 'O Lord, (it is) semen! O Lord, (it is now) a clot (*a glub of blood*)! O Lord, (it is now) a piece of flesh.' And then, if Allah wishes to complete its creation, the angel asks, 'O Lord, (will it be) a male or a female? A wretched (an evil doer) or a blessed (doer of good)? How much will his provisions be? What will his age be?' So all that is written while the creature is still in the mother's womb." *Bukhari 77.594*

In another hadith, the Prophet is clearer as to what timeframe we are talking about here. The following saying may be important for those who would like to see Islam allow early term abortions. If Allah's Messenger says Allah breathes a soul into an embryo 120 days after conception, why not allow abortions until this takes place (whether the angel in the following hadith is the same winged wonder sent to witness the inseminator's ejaculations in the previous saying of the Prophet is a question for scholars).

Narrated Abdullah:

Allah's Apostle, the truthful and truly-inspired, said, "Each one of you collected in the womb of his mother for forty days, and then turns into a clot for an equal period (of forty days) and turns into a piece of flesh for a similar period (of forty days) and then Allah sends an angel and orders him to write four things, i.e. his provision, his age, and whether he will be of the wretched or the blessed (in the Hereafter). Then the soul is breathed into him. And by Allah, a person among you (or a man) may do deeds of the people of the Fire till there is only a cubit or an arm-breadth distance between him and the Fire, but then that writing (which Allah has ordered the angel to write) precedes, and he does the deeds of the people of Paradise and enters it; and a man may do the deeds of the people of Paradise till there is only a cubit or two between him and Paradise, and then that writing precedes and he does the deeds of the people of the Fire and enters it."

Bukhari 77.593

Allah taught His angels how to write your good and bad deeds; therefore, I think it is safe to assume that in the following hadith, it is His angels who do most of the scribbling, not Allah personally.

Narrated Ibn Abbas:

The Prophet narrating about his Lord said, "Allah ordered (the appointed angels over you) that the good and the bad deeds be written, and He then showed (the way) how (to write). If somebody intends to do a good deed and he does not do it, then Allah will write for him a full good deed (in his account with Him); and if he intends to do a good deed and actually did it, then Allah will write for him (in his account) with Him (its reward equal) from ten to seven hundred times to many more times: and if somebody intended to do a bad deed and he does not do it, then Allah will write a full good deed (in his account) with Him, and if he intended to do it (a bad deed) and actually did it, then Allah will write one bad deed (in his account)."

Bukhari 76.498

Perhaps the most important thing some angels ever did was showing the Prophet around Paradise and Hell. God's Messenger's vivid reports about what he saw during these guided tours would not have been possible without the assistance of these selfless fearless guides. One hadith among more than a hundred about these informative out-of-this-world excursions:

Narrated Jabir:

The Prophet, said, "I entered Paradise and saw a palace and asked whose palace is this? They (the Angels) said, This palace belongs to Umar bin Al-Khattab.' I intended to enter it, and nothing stopped me except my knowledge about your sense of Ghira (self-respect (O Umar)."

Umar said, "O Allah's Apostle! Let my father and mother be sacrificed for you! O Allah's Prophet! How dare I think of my Ghira (self-respect) being offended by you?"

Bukhari 62.153

Angels have been known to quarrel among themselves.

Narrated Abu Said Al-Khudri:

The Prophet said, "Amongst the men of Bani (*tribe of*) Israel there was a man who had murdered ninety-nine persons. Then he set out asking (whether his repentance could be accepted or not). He came upon a monk and asked him if his repentance could be accepted. The monk replied in the negative and so the man killed him. He kept on asking till a man advised to go to such and such village. (So he left for it) but death overtook him on the way. While dying, he turned his chest towards that village (where he had hoped his repentance would be accepted), and so the angels of mercy and the angels of punishment quarreled amongst themselves regarding him. Allah ordered the village (towards which he was going) to come closer to him, and ordered the village (whence he had come), to go far away, and then He ordered the angels to measure the distances between his body and the two villages. So he was found to be one span closer to the village (he was going to). So he was forgiven."

Bukhari 56.676

Who watches you not having sex:

Narrated Abu Huraira:

The Prophet said, "If a man invites his wife to sleep with him and she refuses to come to him, then the angels send their curses on her till morning."

Bukhari 62.121

Narrated Abu Huraira:

The Prophet said, "If a woman spends the night deserting her husband's bed (does not sleep with him), then the angels send their curses on her till she comes back (to her husband)."

Bukhari 61.122

If you want angels to show up at your place, get rid of any pictures including cushions with pictures, unless you intend to refuse your husband's advances and don't care to be visited by angels who will curse you while you sleep.

Narrated Aisha:

I purchased a cushion with pictures on it. The Prophet (came and) stood at the door but did not enter. I said (to him), "I repent to Allah for what (the guilt) I have done."

He said, "What is this cushion?"

I said, "It is for you to sit on and recline on."

He said, "The makers of these pictures will be punished on the Day of Resurrection and it will be said to them, 'Make alive what you have created.' Moreover, the angels do not enter a house where there are pictures."

Bukhari 72.840

Apostates Hadiths

Excerpt from:
1,001 Sayings and Deeds of the Prophet Muhammad, Boreal Books

Narrated Abdullah:

Allah's Apostle said, "The blood of a Muslim who confesses that none has the right to be worshipped but Allah and that I am His Apostle, cannot be shed except in three cases: In Qisas (the right of the family of a murder victim to demand the murderer be put to death) for murder, a married person who commits illegal sexual intercourse and the one who reverts from Islam (apostate) and leaves the Muslims."

Bukhari 83.17

Kill those who unconvert (sic) after converting to Islam and those who were born into the *perfect religion* and now would leave it for one less perfect or no religion at all. Is it any wonder Islam has been on a continuous growth curve since its founding?

Kill the apostates, and get a reward!

Narrated Ali:

Whenever I tell you a narration from Allah's Apostle, by Allah, I would rather fall down from the sky than ascribe a false statement to him, but if I tell you something between me and you (not a Hadith) then it was indeed a trick (i.e., I may say things just to cheat my enemy).

No doubt I heard Allah's Apostle saying, "During the last days there will appear some young foolish people who will say the best words but their faith will not go beyond their throats (i.e. they will have no faith) and will go out from (leave) their religion as an arrow goes out from the game.

So, wherever you find them, kill them, for whoever kills them shall have reward on the Day of Resurrection."

Bukhari 84.64

Ali, the Prophet's son-in-law and the fourth caliph (leader of the believers) and second only to his father-in-law in esteem among the Shias, used to burned apostates.

Narrated Ikrima:

Ali burnt some people and this news reached Ibn Abbas, who said, "Had I been in his place I would not have burnt them, as the Prophet said, 'Don't punish (anybody) with Allah's Punishment.'

No doubt, I would have killed them, for the Prophet said, 'If somebody (a Muslim) discards his religion, kill him.'"

Bukhari 52.260

The casual killing of an apostate:

Narrated Abu Burda:

Abu Musa said, "I came to the Prophet along with two men (from the tribe) of Ash'ariyin, one on my right and the other on my left, while Allah's Apostle was brushing his teeth (with a Siwak), and both men asked him for some employment.

The Prophet said, 'O Abu Musa (O Abdullah bin Qais!).'

I said, 'By Him Who sent you with the Truth, these two men did not tell me what was in their hearts and I did not feel (realize) that they were seeking employment.'

As if I were looking now at his Siwak being drawn to a corner under his lips, and he said, 'We never (or, we do not) appoint for our affairs anyone who seeks to be employed. But O Abu Musa! (or Abdullah bin Qais!) go to Yemen.'"

The Prophet then sent Mu'adh bin Jabal (*another companion of the Prophet and one of the most revered scholars of Islam*) after him and when Mu'adh reached him, he spread out a cushion for him and requested him to get down (and sit on the cushion). Behold: There was a fettered man beside Abu Muisa.

Mu'adh asked, "Who is this (man)?"

Abu Muisa said, "He was a Jew and became a Muslim and then reverted back to Judaism."

Then Abu Muisa requested Mu'adh to sit down but Mu'adh said, "I will not sit down till he has been killed. This is the judgment of Allah and His Apostle (for such cases) and repeated it thrice.

Then Abu Musa ordered that the man be killed, and he was killed.

Abu Musa added, "Then we discussed the night prayers and one of us said, 'I pray and sleep, and I hope that Allah will reward me for my sleep as well as for my prayers.'"

Bukhari 84.58

The first person the Prophet ordered killed after the conquest of Mecca was an apostate.

Narrated Anas bin Malik:

Allah's Apostle entered Mecca in the year of its Conquest wearing an Arabian helmet on his head and when the Prophet took it off, a person came and said, "Ibn Khatal is holding the covering of the Ka'ba (taking refuge in the Ka'ba)."

The Prophet said, "Kill him."

Bukhari 29.72

Khatal had been one of the Prophet's Zakat (charity) collectors. He later abandoned Islam and returned to Mecca. He was one of six men and four women God's Messenger ordered assassinated upon taking Mecca. The Prophet, in a rambling hadith which touches on both the sacred and the mundane justified the assassinations. This was after promising the Meccans that he would not harm anyone if the city surrendered without a fight. Allah, it would seem, had consented to suspend His interdiction, if only temporally and only for His Messenger, against killing anyone in the sanctuary that was His City.

Narrated Abu Huraira:

In the year of the Conquest of Mecca, the tribe of Khuza'a killed a man from the tribe of Bani Laith in revenge for a killed person, belonging to them.

They informed the Prophet about it. So he rode his Rahila (she-camel for riding) and addressed the people saying, "Allah held back the killing from Mecca. (The sub-narrator is in doubt whether the Prophet said 'elephant or killing' as the Arabic words standing for these words have great similarity in shape), but He (Allah) let His Apostle and the believers overpower the infidels of Mecca. Beware! (Mecca is a sanctuary) Verily! Fighting in Mecca was not permitted for anyone before me nor will it be permitted for anyone after me. It (war) in it was made legal for me for few hours or so on that day. No doubt it is at this moment a sanctuary, it is not allowed to uproot its thorny shrubs or to uproot its trees or to pick up its Luqatt (fallen things) except by a person who will look for its owner (announce it publicly). And if somebody is killed, then his closest relative has the right to choose one of the two, the blood money (Diyya) or retaliation having the killer killed."

In the meantime a man from Yemen came and said, "O Allah's Apostle! Get that written for me."

The Prophet ordered his companions to write that for him. Then a man from Quraish said, "Except Al-Iqhkhir (a type of grass that has good smell) O Allah's Apostle, as we use it in our houses and graves."

The Prophet said, "Except Al-Iqhkhir. Al-Idhkhir is allowed to be plucked."

Bukhari 3.112

The Unwelcoming Grave

The fantastic story of a Christian who became a Muslim, who became a Christian and then died, and whose body was repeatedly rejected by his grave, is not explicitly attributed to the Prophet, but Bukhari thought it important enough to include in his collection.

Narrated Anas:

There was a Christian who embraced Islam and read Surat-al-Baqara and Al-Imran, and he used to write (the revelations) for the Prophet. Later on he returned to Christianity again and he used to say: "Muhammad knows nothing but what I have written for him."

Then Allah caused him to die, and the people buried him, but in the morning they saw that the earth had thrown his body out. They said, "This is the act of Muhammad and his companions. They dug the grave of our companion and took his body out of it because he had run away from them."

They again dug the grave deeply for him, but in the morning they again saw that the earth had thrown his body out.

They [again] said, "This is an act of Muhammad and his companions. They dug the grave of our companion and threw his body outside it, for he had run away from them."

They dug the grave for him as deep as they could, but in the morning they again saw that the earth had thrown his body out. So they believed that what had befallen him was not done by human beings and had to leave him thrown (on the ground).

Bukhari 56.814

Apostates Koran

Excerpt from:
Getting to Know Allah, Boreal Books

Some modern Islamic scholars, according to Ibn Warraq author of *Why I am not a Muslim* and *Leaving Islam: Apostates Speak Out*, argue that "in the Koran the apostate is threatened with punishment only in the next world".

Warraq disagrees with this interpretation, as do most traditional Islamic scholars; two compelling reasons being verse 4:89 and a hadith from the Prophet Muhammad that demonstrates that when it comes to apostates both Allah and His Messenger are of the same mind, and unequivocally so.

Allah said:

> 4:89 They wish that you disbelieve, as they have disbelieved, so that you will all be alike. Do not, then, take any companions from them, until they emigrate in the Way of Allah. Then should they turn back, seize them and kill them wherever you find them; and do not take from them any companions or supporter;

The Prophet said:

> If a Muslim discards his religion, kill him. (Bukhari: 4.52.260).

In war, deserters are usually executed to deter others from abandoning the fight. Islam, since the Prophet's flight to Medina, year one in the Islamic calendar, has considered itself at war with the unbelievers until such a time as they have all submitted to the Will of Allah or have been killed or enslaved. Allah and His Messenger's demand that those who abandon the Faith, with the outcome of the war still undecided, may have to do with not weakening the war effort as desertions tend to do.

Allah did make at least two exceptions to His general rule of killing apostates "wherever you find them."

> 4:90 Except for those who seek refuge with a people with whom you are bound by a compact, or come to you because their hearts forbid them to fight you or fight their own people. Had Allah wished, He would have made them

dominate you; and then they would have certainly fought you. If, however, they leave you alone and do not fight you and offer you peace, then Allah allows you no way against them.

4:91 You shall find others who wish to be secure from you and secure from their own people; yet whenever they are called back to sedition (polytheism) they plunge into it. If these do not keep away from you, nor offer you peace, nor hold their hands back, then seize them and kill them wherever you find them. Those we have given you clear authority over them.

16:106 He who disbelieves in Allah after He has believed, except him who is compelled, but his heart remains firm in belief (will be forgiven); but those whose hearts rejoice in disbelief shall incur Allah's Wrath and a grievous punishment awaits them.

Apostates may not believe in the Hereafter, but the Hereafter will be waiting, but not in a good way.

16:109 There is no doubt that in the Hereafter they shall be the losers.

Battle of Badr

Excerpt from:

Allah's War Against the Unbelievers, Boreal Books

The Prophet and his followers, after being run out of Mecca, took refuge in Medina from which they attacked the caravans passing between the Red Sea and the oasis city on their way to and from Mecca, igniting a civil war.

Narrated Jabir:

The Prophet sent us as an army unit of three hundred warriors under the command of Abu 'Ubaida to ambush a caravan of the Quraish ...

Bukhari 67.402

The first real battle of what would become a bloody fratricidal war was an attack on a force of an estimated one thousand Meccans sent to protect a large caravan which the Muslims intended to plunder. God's Messenger initially wanted to attack the caravan before the Meccan forces could intervene, but Allah promised him a victory no matter which he chose to attack. With God's guarantee of victory, the Prophet decided on the armed detachment, a decision which did not meet with unanimous approval.

8:5 Just as when your (meaning Muhammad) Lord brought you out in truth from your house (*to fight*), though a group of the believers disliked it.

Moududi quotes a different translation of 8:5 where it's all about the spoils:

8:5 (Now with regard to the spoils the same situation exists as when) your Lord brought you forth from your home in a righteous cause while a party among the believers were much averse to it.

8:6 They disputed with you concerning the Truth after it had become manifest, as though they were being led to their deaths while looking on.

8:7 And [remember] how Allah promised you that one of the two [enemy] groups (the Meccan caravan of Quraysh and the army which was sent to defend it) would be yours, and you wanted the unarmed one (the caravan) to be yours. Allah, however, willed the Truth to triumph in accordance with His Words and to cut off the remnants of the unbelievers.

To avoid His Messenger getting cold feet the night before the battle, in a dream Allah made the enemy appear to be much fewer and repeated the same illusion the next day to a fully awake Prophet.

8:43 [Remember] when Allah showed them to you [O Muhammad] in your sleep as few. Had He showed them to you as many, you would have lost heart and you would have differed over the matter. But Allah saved you. He knows what is hidden in the hearts.

8:44 And [remember] when He showed them to you, as you met, few in your eyes and made you few in their eyes; so that Allah might bring about a matter already decreed. And unto Allah shall all matters return.

The following verse, where the believers saw themselves outnumbered two to one, makes sense if only the Prophet was subjected to the illusion of a small Meccan army:

3:13 There surely was a sign for you in the two armies that confronted each other (at the Battle of Badr); the one side fighting for the cause of Allah, and the other consisting of unbelievers. The believers saw them with their very eyes to be twice their actual number. God will strengthen with His Might whomever He pleases. Surely, there is in this a lesson for those who are possessed of vision.

The Mohsin Khan Translation disputes Allah's estimate, making it 3 to 1, and the sign was for the Jews.

3:13 There has already been a sign for you (O Jews) in the two armies that met (in combat i.e. the Battle of Badr). One was fighting in the Cause of Allah, and as for the other, (they) were disbelievers. They (the believers) saw them (the disbelievers) with their own eyes twice their number (although they were thrice their number). And Allah supports with His Victory whom He wills. Verily, in this is a lesson for those who understand.

No matter their relative strength, the believers held the high ground. They would have abandoned that strategic position and attacked the caravan ("cavalcade" in revelation 8:42), with disastrous result, had Allah not already decided how the battle would unfold and why.

> 8:42 While you were on the nearer side [of the valley] and they were on the farther side, with the cavalcade beneath you. Had you made an appointment, you would surely have failed to keep the appointment. But [this happened] so that Allah might bring about a matter already decreed, and that those who were to perish would perish after a clear proof [had been given], and those who were to survive would survive after a clear proof [had been given]. And surely Allah is All-Hearing, All-Knowing.

The Muslim defeated the Meccans at the famous battle of Badr with Allah taking credit for the victory.

> 8:8 So that He may cause the Truth to triumph and nullify falsehood, even though the wicked sinner dislike it.

And why shouldn't He. After all, He did send an army of invisible angels to help the Muslims defeat their enemy, and made it possible for the believers to fall asleep, in an uncharacteristic rain, the night before the battle.

> 8:9 And when you called upon your Lord for help, He answered you: "I will re-enforced you with a thousand angels following one another."

> 8:10 Allah did this only as good tidings and that your hearts might be assured thereby. Victory comes from Allah; Allah is indeed Mighty and Wise.

> 8:11 [Remember] when He allowed slumber to overcome you as an assurance from Him, and sent you water down from heaven so as to purify you, relieve you of the Devil's temptation, fortify your hearts and steady your feet therewith.

Words of encouragement for His angels:

> 8:12 And when your Lord revealed to the angels: "I am with you; so support those who believe. I will cast terror into the hearts of those who disbelieve; so strike upon the necks and strike every fingertip of theirs."

> 8:13 That is because they opposed Allah and His Messenger; and he who opposes Allah and His Messenger [will find] Allah's Punishment very severe.

8:14 This is how it will be; so taste it; the torture of the Fire is awaiting the unbelievers.

Words of encouragement for the believers:

8:15 O believers, if you meet the unbelievers on the march, do not turn your backs upon them.

8:16 Whoever turns his back on that day, unless preparing to resume fighting, or joining another group, incurs Allah's Wrath and his refuge is Hell; and what an evil fate!

8:45 O believers, if you encounter an enemy host, stand fast and remember Allah frequently, that perchance you may prosper.

8:46 And obey Allah and His Messenger and do not quarrel among yourselves lest you lose heart and your strength dissipates. And stand fast, for Allah is on the side of those who stand fast.

8:47 And do not be like those who went out of their homes boastfully showing off in front of the people, while they barred others from the Path of Allah. Allah is fully aware of what they do.

"[8:47] alludes to the army of the disbelieving Quraysh, which, when it proceeded on a military expedition against the Muslims, was accompanied by singing and dancing minstrels." *Moududi*

Words of encouragement from Satan for the unbelievers – the Devil fled the battlefield before any actual engagement, which probably demoralized the opponents of the believers somewhat.

8:48 And the Devil made their [foul] deeds look fair to them saying: "No man shall overcome you today; and I am indeed by your side." But when the two hosts sighed each other, he turned on his heels saying: "I am quit of you; I see what you do not see; I fear Allah, and Allah is stern in retribution."

What about the hypocrites?

8:49 And the hypocrites and those in whose hearts is a sickness said: "Their religion has misled those people (the Muslims)." But he who trusts in Allah will find Allah is Mighty and Wise.

Strong winds lashed the battlefield. One wind blast, the Prophet told his fighters, was one thousand angels led by the archangel Gabriel coming to their aid. The next blast, he said, was another thousand angels led by the archangel Michael. A third was still another thousand angels led by the archangel Saraphel.

Allah gives details of this re-enforcement from heaven, but not before reminding the faithful of the second encounter between the Muslims and the Meccans at the Battle of Uhud (March 19, 625).

> 3:123 Allah had already given you victory at Badr, at a time when you were still powerless; so fear Allah that perchance you might thankful.

> 3:124 When you (*Muhammad*) were telling the believers: "Is it not enough that your Lord should reinforce you with three thousand angels sent down?"

Even with the assistance of three thousand angels, the Prophet's men could not defeat the Meccans. Allah had to send another two thousand angels (unless these angels were held in reserve and the battle was won without their assistance) bringing the total number of winged combatants the Almighty committed to the Battle of Badr to five thousand.

> 3:125 Yes, if you forbear and fear Allah and the enemy attack you at once, Your Lord will reinforce you with five thousand marked angels.

> 3:126 Allah has not intended this except as good news to you and that your hearts might be reassured thereby. Victory comes only from Allah, the Mighty, the Wise.

Gabriel was proud of the way his angels fought, and he may also have been the only mounted warrior at the battle of Badr.

Narrated Rifaa: (who was one of the Badr warriors)

Gabriel came to the Prophet and said, "How do you look upon the warriors of Badr among yourselves?"

The Prophet said, "As the best of the Muslims." or said a similar statement.

On that, Gabriel said, "And so are the Angels who participated in the Badr (battle)."

Bukhari 59.327

Narrated Ibn Abbas:

The Prophet said on the day (of the battle) of Badr, "This is Gabriel holding the head of his horse and equipped with arms for the battle.

Bukhari 59.330

The angels were not only there to fight, but also to carry the souls of the dead unbelievers to Hell.

8:50 And if you could only see when the angels carry off the unbelievers, striking their faces and their rears [saying]: "Taste the punishment of the Fire."

8:51 That is on account of what you have done, and Allah is not unjust to His servants.

The total number of enemy dead at the Battle of Badr was 70, and, as Allah reminds the believers, it was not they who slew them.

8:17 It was not you who slew them, but Allah; and when you (Muhammad) threw (a handful of dust in the direction of the enemy) it was actually Allah who threw; so that He might generously reward the believers. Allah is All-Hearing, All-Knowing.

Narrated Al-Bara bin Azib:

On the day of Uhud the Prophet appointed Abdullah bin Jubair as chief of the archers, and seventy among us were injured and martyred. On the day (of the battle) of Badr, the Prophet and his companions had inflicted 140 casualties on the pagans, 70 were taken prisoners, and 70 were killed.

Bukhari 56.322

Why Allah threw the dust:

8:18 That was done, so that Allah might foil the machinations of the unbelievers.

The Prophet had one of his most vocal critics, the poet al-Nadr whom he spotted after the battle, killed on the spot, but he did show mercy to sixty or more other prisoners. He ignored demands that each be killed by a relative to avoid a blood feud and a demand that they be burnt alive, and ordered that they be ransomed. He was exercising Allah's prerogative.

3:127 That He may cut off a group of the unbelievers or humiliate them, so that they may turn away completely baffled.

3:128 It is no business of yours whether Allah forgives them or punishes them; for they are indeed evil-doers!

3:129 And to Allah belongs what is in the heavens and on earth; He forgives whom He pleases and punishers whom He pleases. Allah is All-Forgiving and Merciful.

Where some of the Muslim dead are, and why it all makes sense.

Narrated Anas:

Haritha was martyred on the day (of the battle) of Badr, and he was a young boy then. His mother came to the Prophet and said, "O Allah's Apostle! You know how dear Haritha is to me. If he is in Paradise, I shall remain patient, and hope for reward from Allah, but if it is not so, then you shall see what I do?"

He said, "May Allah be merciful to you! Have you lost your senses? Do you think there is only one Paradise? There are many Paradises and your son is in the (most superior) Paradise of Al-Firdaus."

Bukhari 59.318

Dead pagans down the well and booty for the believers.

Narrated Ibn Shihab:

These were the battles of Allah's Apostle (which he fought), and while mentioning (the Badr battle) he said, while the corpses of the pagans were being thrown into the well, Allah's Apostle said (to them), "Have you found what your Lord promised true?"

Abdullah said, "Some of the Prophet's companions said, "O Allah's Apostle! You are addressing dead people.'"

Allah's Apostle replied, "You do not hear what I am saying, better than they."

The total number of Muslim fighters from Quraish who fought in the battle of Badr and were given their share of the booty, were 81 men."

Az-Zubair said, "When their shares were distributed, their number was 101 men. But Allah knows it better."

Bukhari 59.360

None of the victorious warriors of the battle of Badr survived the upheaval that followed the assassination of the third caliph.

Narrated Said bin Al-Musaiyab:

When the first civil strife (in Islam) took place because of the murder of Uthman, it left none of the Badr warriors alive.

When the second civil strife, that is the battle of Al-Harra, took place, it left none of the Hudaibiya treaty companions alive.

Then the third civil strife took place and it did not subside till it had exhausted all the strength of the people.

Bukhari 59.358

Cain and Abel

Excerpt from:
Shared Prophets, Boreal Books

Of all the stories from the Bible that have found their way into the Koran, the story of Cain and Abel is probably one of the most significant for both Christians and Muslims. Allah, with this story about brother killing brother (the Koran does not mention Adam's two sons by name), establishes a fundamental difference between the teachings of Jesus of Nazareth and His Revelations. Where Jesus said to turn the other cheek, Allah countered with repay a wrong done to you in kind and a wrong done to Me, or my Messenger, in spades.

> 2:179 In retaliation there is life for you, O people of understanding, that you may be God-fearing.

> 5:33 Indeed, the punishment of those who fight Allah and His Messenger and go around corrupting the land is to be killed, crucified, have their hands and feet cut off on opposite sides, or to be banished from the land. That is a disgrace for them in this life, and in the life to come theirs will be a terrible punishment.

We take up the story of Cain and Abel after Allah has asked Moses to tell this cautionary tale to his unruly followers whom He has condemned to wander the desert for forty years for refusing to enter the Promised Land because they feared its inhabitants (see *Moses at the Gates of the Promised Land*).

> 5:27 And recite to them in all truth the tale of Adam's two sons, when they offered a sacrifice, which was accepted from one, but not accepted from the other. The latter said: "I will surely kill you", the other replied: "Allah accepts only from the God-fearing.

> 5:28 "Should you stretch your hand out to kill me, I will not stretch my hand out to kill you; for I fear Allah, Lord of the Worlds.

> 5:29 "I only wish that you be charged with my sin and yours and thus be one of the companions of the Fire; and that is the reward of the evildoers."

> 5:30 Then his soul prompted him to kill his brother; and so he killed him and became one of the losers.

5:31 Then Allah sent forth a raven digging the earth to show him how to bury his brother's corpse. He said: "Woe is me, am I unable to be like this raven and bury the corpse of my brother?" Thus he became one of the remorseful.

Law of Retaliation

With the murder of Abel, Allah confirms that the Law of Retaliation i.e. talion law is the law of the land where murder is concerned.

> 5:32 For that reason, We decreed for the Children of Israel that whoever kills a soul, not in retaliation for a soul or corruption in the land, is like one who has killed the whole of mankind; and whoever saves a life is like one who saves the lives of all mankind. Our Messengers came to them with the clear proofs; but afterwards many of them continued to commit excesses in the land.

To limit these excesses may be why Allah imposed a slaying limit on retaliatory murders.

> 17:33 Do not kill the soul which Allah has forbidden except for a just cause. Whoever is killed unjustly, We have given his heir the power [to demand satisfaction]; but let him not exceed the limit in slaying, for he will be the victor.

After the attacks of 9/11, Muslim community leaders said that those who caused the deaths of thousands in New York, Washington and Pennsylvania were not true Muslims because in verse 5:32 Allah said that "whoever kills a soul is like killing all of mankind", therefore no Muslim could have done this. Conveniently leaving out the part about a person who kills another is not "like one who has killed all of mankind" if the murder is in retaliation for a previous murder, or a real or perceived wrong done to Allah or His Messenger i.e. corruption of the land.

President Bush, Prime Minister Blair, journalists, Islamic scholars and others echoed this "politically correct fabrication" according to the Chairman of the British National Party "to avoid an explosion of hostility against Muslims" by leaving the impression that the central message of the Koran is all about peace and love; that "Islam... is Christianity with a towel on its head."

Retaliation is a central theme of the Koran: brutal retaliation if the alleged crime is deemed to be a crime against Allah or His Messenger, proportionate retaliation for wrongs done to the believers and sometimes, perhaps not often enough, forgiveness.

Fight evil with evil, and perhaps not, if it will lead to the reforming of the wrongdoer i.e. he becomes a believer.

42:40 The reward of evil is an evil like it, but he who pardons and makes amends, his wage is with Allah. Indeed, He does not like the wrongdoers.

Moududi's comments (partial):

Although it is permissible to retaliate against the one who has committed violence, wherever pardoning can be conducive to reconcilement, pardoning is better for the sake of reconcilement than retaliation. And since man pardons the other by suppressing his own feelings, Allah says that the reward of such a one is with Him, for he has suppressed his own self for the sake of reforming the evil-doers.

Should you still decide to retaliate in kind, it will not be held against you.

42:41 He who overcomes after being wronged – upon those there is no reproach.

42:42 The reproach is surely upon those who wrong mankind and transgress in the land unjustly. To those a painful punishment is in store.

42:43 Be he who bears patiently and forgives – that is a sign of real resolve.

It is unfortunate that, more often than not, Allah follows resounding moral declarations, such as forgiving, with a brutal reminder that these are meant for co-religionists only; and, notwithstanding what I have just said, there are other conditions you must meet before I give you the keys to Paradise, dying while killing unbelievers being one of them for some (revelations 3:140-142).

3:137 There have been examples (of how Allah dealt with the unbelievers) before you; so travel in the land and behold the fate of those who disbelieved.

3:138 This is a declaration for mankind, a guidance and admonition for the God-fearing.

3:139 Do not be faint-hearted and do not grieve; you will have the upper hand, if you are true believers.

3:140 If you have been afflicted by a wound, a similar wound has afflicted the others (the unbelievers). Such are the times; We alternate them among the people, so that Allah may know who are the believers and choose martyrs from among you. Allah does not like the evildoers!

3:141 And that Allah might purify the believers and annihilate the unbelievers.

3:142 Or did you suppose that you will enter Paradise, before Allah has known who were those of you who have struggled, and those who are steadfast.

3:143 You were yearning for death before you actually met it. Now you have seen it and you are beholding it.

Dead Poets

Excerpt from:
1,001 Sayings and Deeds of the Prophet Muhammad, Boreal Books

Allah said to "kill them wherever you find them"! Nowhere was this truer than for the poets who lampooned the Prophet or whom people thought better at writing rhythm and rhyme than His Messenger. In their murder the Prophet took a personal interest.

The first poet to be killed was al-Nadr. The Meccans had praised his verses as superior to those of the Prophet and this had enraged the perfect human being. When God's Messenger spotted al-Nadr among the prisoners captured at Badr he had him beheaded on the spot. Next to die was the poetess Asma bint Marwan. She was stabbed to death while sleeping with an infant suckling at her breast. Her murder was followed by that of the Jewish poet Abu Afak who was also killed while he slept.

> He waited for an opportunity until a hot night came, and Abu Afak slept in an open place. Salim b. Umayr knew it, so he placed the sword on his liver and pressed it till it reached his bed. The enemy of Allah screamed and the people, who were his followers rushed him, took him to his house and interred him.
>
> *Ibn S'ad, a companion of the Prophet*

> After every murder the assassin would go to the Mosque to inform God's Messenger and be praised for what they had done at his insistence. For example, the killer of Asma bint Marwan had just entered the building when the Prophet asked him "Have you slain the daughter of Marwan?"

> This was the word that was first heard from the Apostle of Allah, may Allah bless him. When Umayr replied that the job had been carried out with success, Muhammad said, "You have helped God and His apostle, O Umayr!'"

> When Umayr asked if he would have to bear any evil consequences, the apostle said, "Two goats won't butt their heads about her."

Muhammad then praised Umayr in front of all gathered for prayer for his act of murder, and Umayr went back to his people.

Ibn S'ad

The call for the murder of the poet Ka'b bin Al-Ashraf:

Narrated Jabir bin Abdullah:

Allah's Apostle said, "Who would kill Ka'b bin Al-Ashraf (Ka'b, a poet, who wrote poems lampooning of Allan's Messenger) as he has harmed Allah and His Apostle?"

Muhammad bin Maslama (got up and) said, "I will kill him."

So, Muhammad bin Maslama went to Ka'b and said, "I want a loan of one or two Wasqs of food grains."

Ka'b said, "Mortgage your women to me."

Muhammad bin Maslama said, "How can we mortgage our women, and you are the most handsome among the Arabs?"

He said, "Then mortgage your sons to me."

Muhammad said, "How can we mortgage our sons, as the people will abuse them for being mortgaged for one or two Wasqs of food grains? It is shameful for us. But we will mortgage our arms to you."

So, Muhammad bin Maslama promised him that he would come to him next time. They (Muhammad bin Maslama and his companions came to him as promised and murdered him. Then they went to the Prophet and told him about it.

Bukhari 45.687

The murder of the poet Abu Rafi:

Narrated Al-Bara bin Azib:

Allah's Apostle sent a group of Ansari men to kill Abu-Rafi. One of them set out and entered their (i.e. the enemies) fort. That man said, "I hid myself in a stable for their animals. They closed the fort gate. Later they lost a donkey of theirs, so they went out in its search. I, too, went out along with them, pretending to look for it. They found the donkey and entered their fort. And I, too, entered along with them.

They closed the gate of the fort at night, and kept its keys in a small window where I could see them. When those people slept, I took the keys and opened the gate of the fort and came upon Abu Rafi and said, 'O Abu Rafi.'

When he replied me, I proceeded towards the voice and hit him. He shouted and I came out to come back, pretending to be a helper.

I said, 'O Abu Rafi, changing the tone of my voice.'

He asked me, 'What do you want; woe to your mother?'

I asked him, 'What has happened to you?'

He said, 'I don't know who came to me and hit me.' Then I drove my sword into his belly and pushed it forcibly till it touched the bone. Then I came out, filled with puzzlement and went towards a ladder of theirs in order to get down but I fell down and sprained my foot.

I came to my companions and said, 'I will not leave till I hear the wailing of the women.'

So, I did not leave till I heard the women bewailing Abu Rafi, the merchant of Hijaz. Then I got up, feeling no ailment, (and we proceeded) till we came upon the Prophet and informed him."

Bukhari 52.264

The man who wanted to be known for his poetry would end up hating the genre and its practitioners.

Narrated Ibn Umar:

The Prophet said, "It is better for a man to fill the inside of his body with pus than to fill it with poetry."

Bukhari 73.175

Destruction of the Christian Mosque of Medina

Excerpt from:

Allah's War Against the Unbelievers, Boreal Books

It was on the return journey from Tabuk that Allah revealed to His Messenger what He thought about the mosque built by the Christian monk Abu 'Amir al Rahib, and those who prayed there.

The Masjid al-Dirar had been built next to the Masjid al-Quba whose first stones were positioned by the Prophet himself. After receiving the revelation that He should not pray there, God's Messenger realized that it had been a mistake to allow its construction and had the Masjid al-Dirar destroyed. The fact that the Christian mosque was built with the Prophet's approval would indicate that Abu Amir's intentions were honourable, but revelation 9:107 says otherwise.

> 9:107 And those who build a mosque (the reference is to the mosque built in the neighbourhood of the mosque of Quba', the first mosque built by Muslims with the Prophet helping out) or hurt [the Muslims], to spread unbelief, to disunite [the believers] and to await him (he is said to be Abu 'Amir) who had fought Allah and His Messenger – they will certainly swear that they meant nothing but good. Allah bears witness that they are liars.

> 9:108 Do not stand up there [for prayer]; for a mosque founded on piety from the first day is worthier of you standing in it. Therein are men who love to be purified; and Allah loves those who purify themselves.

What could pass for a parable:

> 9:109 Is one who founds his edifice upon the fear and Good Pleasure of Allah better, or one who founds his edifice upon the brink of a crumbling precipice that will tumble down with him into the Fire of Hell? Allah does not guide the unjust people.

> 9:110 The edifice which they built will continue to be a source of doubt in their hearts, unless their hearts are cut up into pieces. Allah is All-Knowing, Wise.

Dreams

(partial)

Excerpt from:

1,001 Sayings and Deeds of the Prophet Muhammad, Boreal Books

The Koran is all over the place as to when it was revealed. In one instance, it is during one night, the night of power (97:1); in another it is during an entire month, the month of Ramadan (2:185); and in still another instance, it was revealed "piecemeal" (17:106). Nowhere in His Book does Allah mention revealing what He revealed of His Koran in dreams; yet, this is how the Prophet's companions remember God's Messenger receiving many of God's communications, most if not all, from the angel Gabriel, Allah's Messenger to the Messenger.

Narrated Safwan bin Ya'la bin Umaiya from his father who said:

"A man came to the Prophet while he was at Ji'rana. The man was wearing a cloak which had traces of Khaluq or Sufra (a kind of perfume). The man asked (the Prophet), 'What do you order me to perform in my Umra (*the lesser pilgrimage*)?' So, Allah inspired the Prophet divinely and he was screened by a place of cloth.

I wished to see the Prophet being divinely inspired.

Umar said to me, 'Come! Will you be pleased to look at the Prophet while Allah is inspiring him?'

I replied in the affirmative.

Umar lifted one corner of the cloth and I looked at the Prophet who was snoring. (The sub-narrator thought that he said: The snoring was like that of a camel).

When that state was over, the Prophet asked, "Where is the questioner who asked about Umra? Put off your cloak and wash away the traces of Khaluq from your body and clean the Sufra (yellow color) and perform in your Umra what you perform in your Hajj (i.e. the Tawaf round the Ka'ba and the Sa'i between Safa and Marwa)."

Bukhari 27.17

Communications from Paradise sent while the Prophet slept would explain the horrific descriptions of Judgement Day and Hell which mere words could not have conveyed. Aisha, the Prophet's child-bride and the most trusted of the narrators of what God's Messenger said and did remembered her husband receiving "(the Devine Inspiration) in the form of true dreams in his sleep."

Narrated Aisha:

The commencement (of the Divine Inspiration) to Allah's Apostle was in the form of true dreams in his sleep, for he never had a dream but it turned out to be true and clear as the bright daylight. Then he began to like seclusions, so he used to go in seclusion in the cave of Hira where he used to worship Allah continuously for many nights before going back to his family to take the necessary provision (of food) for the stay.

Bukhari 60.478

Dreams, the Prophet explained, convey religious knowledge. What is the Koran if not religious knowledge?

Narrated Ibn Umar:

I heard Allah's Apostle saying, "While I was sleeping, I was given a bowl full of milk (in a dream), and I drank of it to my fill until I noticed its wetness coming out of my nails, and then I gave the rest of it to Umar."

They (the people) asked, "What have you interpreted (about the dream) O Allah's Apostle?"

He said, "(It is Religious) knowledge."

Bukhari 87.134

And what is Islam, if not "The Religion"!

Narrated Abu Sa'id Al-Khudri:

Allah's Apostle said, "While I was sleeping, some people were displayed before me (in a dream). They were wearing shirts, some of which were merely covering their breasts, and some a bit longer. Then there passed before me, Umar bin Al-Khattab wearing a shirt he was dragging it (on the ground behind him.)"

They (the people) asked, "What have you interpreted (about the dream) O Allah's Apostle?"

He said, "The Religion."

Bukhari 87.136

Interpreting dreams as real-world predictions is very much what a Prophet does.

Narrated Abu Huraira:

I heard Allah's Apostle saying, "Nothing is left of the prophetism except Al-Mubashshirat."

They asked, "What are Al-Mubashshirat?"

He replied, "The true good dreams (that conveys glad tidings)."

Bukhari 87.119

None dared wake up the Prophet less he interrupt a transmission from Paradise.

Narrated Imran:

Once we were traveling with the Prophet and we carried on traveling till the last part of the night and then we (halted at a place) and slept (deeply). There is nothing sweeter than sleep for a traveler in the last part of the night. So it was only the heat of the sun that made us to wake up and the first to wake up was so and so, then so and so and then so and so (the narrator Auf said that Abu Raja had told him their names but he had forgotten them) and the fourth person to wake up was Umar bin Al-Khattab.

And whenever the Prophet used to sleep, nobody would wake him up till he himself used to get up as we did not know what was happening (being revealed) to him in his sleep ...

Bukhari 7.340

Nothing gets Allah's and His Messenger's dander up like the mention of paying interest, therefore the Prophet having dreams where riba-eaters figure prominently is to be expected.

Narrated Samura bin Jundab:

The Prophet said, "This night I dreamt that two men came and took me to a Holy land whence we proceeded on till we reached a river of blood, where a man was standing, and on its bank was standing another man with stones in his hands. The man in the middle of the river tried to come out, but the other threw a stone in his mouth and forced him to go back to his original place. So, whenever he tried to come out, the other man would throw a stone in his mouth and force him to go back to his former place."

I asked, "Who is this?"

I was told, "The person in the river was a Riba-eater (*a lender who insist on charging interest on borrowed money*)."

Bukhari 34.298

It was in a dream that the Prophet was given the keys to the treasures of the earth.

Narrated Abu Huraira:

The Prophet said, "I have been given the keys of eloquent speech and given victory with awe (cast into the hearts of the enemy), and while I was sleeping last night, the keys of the treasures of the earth were brought to me till they were put in my hand."

Abu Huraira added: "Allah's Apostle left (this world) and now you people are carrying those treasures from place to place."

Bukhari 87.127

Unless God's Messenger was a somnambulist and fixed himself a snack while in REM sleep, in dreams you can have real food and drinks if you are a Prophet, or important enough to have your dreams catered.

Narrated Abu Sa'id:

That he had heard the Prophet saying, "Do not fast continuously (practise Al-Wisal), and if you intend to lengthen your fast, then carry it on only till the Suhur (before the following dawn)."

The people said to him, "But you practice (Al-Wisal), O Allah's Apostle!"

He replied, "I am not similar to you, for during my sleep I have One Who makes me eat and drink."

Bukhari 31.184

It was fortunate that the crescent moon marking the first day of the month of Shawwal, meaning "lift or carry" (so named because this is the month she-camels normally would be carrying a fetus) appeared when it did, or some believers whose dreams were not being catered and who wanted to fast like their Prophet might have starved themselves to death. The first day of Shawwal is the feast of Eid al-Fitr where all fasting must stop.

Narrated Abu Huraira:

Allah's Apostle forbade Al-Wisal in fasting. So, one of the Muslims said to him, "But you practice Al-Wisal. O Allah's Apostle!"

The Prophet replied, "Who amongst you is similar to me? I am given food and drink during my sleep by my Lord."

So, when the people refused to stop Al-Wisal (fasting continuously), the Prophet fasted day and night continuously along with them for a day and then another day and then they saw the crescent moon (of the month of Shawwal).

The Prophet said to them (angrily), "If it (the crescent) had not appeared, I would have made you fast for a longer period."

That was as a punishment for them when they refused to stop (practising Al-Wisal).

Bukhari 31.186

The difference between a dream and a nightmare:

Narrated Abu Qatada:

The Prophet said, "A true good dream is from Allah, and a bad dream is from Satan."

Bukhari 87.113

Next time you have a nightmare, the Prophet recommends you don't mention it to anyone.

Narrated Abu Sa'id Al-Khudri:

The Prophet said, "If anyone of you sees a dream that he likes, then it is from Allah, and he should thank Allah for it and narrate it to others; but if he sees something else, i.e., a dream that he dislikes, then it is from Satan, and he should seek refuge with Allah from its evil, and he should not mention it to anybody, for it will not harm him."

Bukhari 87.114

When waking up from a bad dream, spit or blow your nose three times.

Narrated Abu Qatada:

The Prophet said, "A good dream that comes true is from Allah, and a bad dream is from Satan, so if anyone of you sees a bad dream, he should seek refuge with Allah from Satan and should spit on the left, for the bad dream will not harm him."

Bukhari 87.115

Perhaps as precaution against spraying saliva on a person next to you in bed and making a bad dream even worse, the Prophet recommended it be a dry spit, maybe just even clearing your throat.

Narrated Abu Qatada:

The Prophet said, "A good dream is from Allah, and a bad dream is from Satan. So whoever has seen (in a dream) something he dislike, then he should spit without saliva, thrice on his left and seek refuge with Allah from Satan, for it will not harm him, and Satan cannot appear in my shape."

Bukhari 87.124

Waking up from a nightmare about Gog and Magog:

Narrated Zainab bint Jahsh:

The Prophet got up from his sleep with a flushed red face and said, "None has the right to be worshipped but Allah. Woe to the Arabs, from the Great evil that is nearly approaching them. Today a gap has been made in the wall of Gog and Magog like this." (Sufyan illustrated by this forming the number 90 or 100 with his fingers.)

It was asked, "Shall we be destroyed though there are righteous people among us?"

The Prophet said, "Yes, if evil increased."

Bukhari 88.181

It is from lucid visions and from a dream of the Prophet that we have the only known eyewitness description of what Jesus looked like.

Narrated Abdullah bin Umar:

Allah's Apostle said, "I saw myself (in a dream) near the Ka'ba last night, and I saw a man with whitish red complexion, the best you may see amongst men of that complexion having long hair reaching his earlobes which was the best hair of its sort, and he had combed his hair and water was dropping from it, and he was performing the Tawaf around the Ka'ba while he was leaning on two men or on the shoulders of two men.

I asked, 'Who is this man?'

Somebody replied, '(He is) Messiah, son of Mary.'

Then I saw another man with very curly hair, blind in the right eye which looked like a protruding out grape. I asked, 'Who is this?'

Somebody replied, '(He is the false) Messiah, Ad-Dajjal.'"

Bukhari 72.789

Communications from Allah via dreams sometimes included visions of good and bad things.

Narrated Um Salama:

The Prophet woke up and said, "Glorified be Allah: What great (how many) treasures have been sent down, and what great (how many) afflictions have been sent down!"

Bukhari 87.128

Many who had dreams where the Prophet was a figurant were not sure if it was God's Messenger who was paying them a visit while they slept, or Satan. The Prophet assured them that it could not be Satan and why.

Narrated Anas:

The Prophet said, "Whoever has seen me in a dream, then no doubt, he has seen me, for Satan cannot imitate my shape."

Bukhari 87.123

The Prophet told his male followers not to name themselves after his first-born son (who died in infancy), followed by another reminder that Satan cannot take his shape in a dream. I could only conjecture what one has to do with the other.

Narrated Abu Huraira:

The Prophet said, "Name yourselves after me (by my name), but do not call yourselves by my Kuniya (*part of an Arabic name which usually begins with "abu" and refers to a father's first-born son*), and whoever sees me in a dream, he surely sees me, for Satan cannot impersonate me (appear in my figure). And whoever intentionally ascribes something to me falsely, he will surely take his place in the (Hell) Fire."

Bukhari 73.217

If enough ordinary men have the same dream then it has to be true.

Narrated Ibn Umar:

Some men amongst the companions of the Prophet were shown in their dreams that the night of Qadr (Night of Power) was in the last seven nights of Ramadan.

Allah's Apostle said, "It seems that all your dreams agree that (the Night of Qadr) is in the last seven nights, and whoever wants to search for it (i.e. the Night of Qadr) should search in the last seven (nights of Ramadan)."

Bukhari 32.232

The reward of true belief as revealed in a dream:

Narrated Abu Musa:

The Prophet said, "In a dream I saw myself migrating from Mecca to a place having plenty of date trees. I thought that it was Al-Yamama or Hajar, but it came to be Medina i.e. Yathrib. In the same dream I saw myself moving a sword and its blade got broken. It came to symbolize the defeat which the Muslims suffered from, on the Day of Uhud. I moved the sword again, and it became normal as before, and that was the symbol of the victory Allah bestowed upon Muslims and their gathering together. I saw cows in my dream, and by Allah, that was a blessing, and they symbolized the believers on the Day of Uhud. And the blessing was the good Allah bestowed upon us and the reward of true belief which Allah gave us after the day of Badr."

Bukhari 56.818

The reward was of course the booty, but I digress. Be careful what you wish for!

Narrated Anas bin Malik:

Allah's Apostle used to visit Um Haram bint Milhan she was the wife of Ubada bin As-Samit. One day the Prophet visited her and she provided him with food and started looking for lice in his head. Then Allah's Apostle slept and afterwards woke up smiling. Um Haram asked, "What makes you smile, O Allah's Apostle?"

He said, "Some of my followers were presented before me in my dream as fighters in Allah's Cause, sailing in the middle of the seas like kings on the thrones or like kings sitting on their thrones." (The narrator Ishaq is not sure as to which expression was correct).

Um Haram added, I said, "O Allah's Apostle! Invoke Allah, to make me one of them."

So Allah's Apostle invoked Allah for her and then laid his head down (and slept). Then he woke up smiling (again). (Um Haram added): I said, "What makes you smile, O Allah's Apostle?"

He said, "Some people of my followers were presented before me (in a dream) as fighters in Allah's Cause."

He said the same as he had said before.

I said, "O Allah's Apostle! Invoke Allah to make me one of them." He said, "You are among the first ones."

Then Um Haram sailed over the sea during the Caliphate of Muawiya bin Abu Sufyan, and she fell down from her riding animal after coming ashore, and died.

Bukhari 87.130

Before Freud, there was the Prophet Muhammad:

Narrated Abdullah bin Salam:

(In a dream) I saw myself in a garden, and there was a pillar in the middle of the garden, and there was a handhold at the top of the pillar. I was asked to climb it. I said, "I cannot." Then a servant came and lifted up my clothes and I climbed (the pillar), and then got hold of the handhold, and I woke up while still holding it.

I narrated that to the Prophet who said, "The garden symbolizes the garden of Islam, and the handhold is the firm Islamic handhold which indicates that you will be adhering firmly to Islam until you die."

Bukhari 87.142

Narrated Abdullah:

The Prophet said, "I saw (in a dream) a black woman with unkempt hair going out of Medina and settling at Mahai'a, i.e., Al-Juhfa. I interpreted that as a symbol of epidemic of Medina being transferred to that place (Al-Juhfa)."

Bukhari 87.161

You did not swear if you wanted the Prophet to let you know what you got wrong in interpreting a dream. It may also have been his way of avoiding giving an explanation.

Narrated Ibn Abbas:

A man came to Allah's Apostle and said, "I saw in a dream, a cloud having shade. Butter and honey were dropping from it and I saw the people gathering it in their hands, some gathering much and some a little. And behold, there was a rope extending from the earth to the sky, and I saw that you (the Prophet) held it and went up, and then another man held it and went up and (after that) another (third) held it and went up, and then after another (fourth) man held it, but it broke and then got connected again."

Abu Bakr said, "O Allah's Apostle! Let my father be sacrificed for you! Allow me to interpret this dream."

The Prophet said to him, "Interpret it."

Abu Bakr said, "The cloud with shade symbolizes Islam, and the butter and honey dropping from it, symbolizes the Quran, its sweetness dropping and some people learning much of the Qur'an and some a little. The rope which is extended from the sky to the earth is the Truth which you (the Prophet) are following. You follow it and Allah will raise you high with it, and then another man will follow it and will rise up with it and another person will follow it and then another man will follow it but it will break and then it will be connected for him and he will rise up with it. O Allah's Apostle! Let my father be sacrificed for you! Am I right or wrong?"

The Prophet replied, "You are right in some of it and wrong in some."

Abu Bakr said, "O Allah's Prophet! By Allah, you must tell me in what I was wrong."

The Prophet said, "Do not swear."

Bukhari 87.170

When your dreams will come true:

Narrated Abu Huraira:

Allah's Apostle said, "When the Day of Resurrection approaches, the dreams of a believer will hardly fail to come true, and a dream of a believer is one of forty-six parts of prophetism, and whatever belongs to prothetism can never be false."

Bukhari 87.144

The worst lie you can tell is about a dream you have not dreamt.

Narrated Ibn Umar:

Allah's Apostle said, "The worst lie is that a person claims to have seen a dream which he has not seen."

Bukhari 87.167

Whatever you do, don't lie about having a dream unless you have very nimble fingers which will be put to the test on Judgement Day.

Narrated Ibn Abbas:

The Prophet said, "Whoever claims to have seen a dream which he did not see, will be ordered to make a knot between two barley grains which he will not be able to do; and if somebody listens to the talk of some people who do not like him (to listen) or they run away from him, then molten lead will be poured into his ears on the Day of Resurrection; and whoever makes a picture, will be punished on the Day of Resurrection and will be ordered to put a soul in that picture, which he will not be able to do."

Bukhari 87.165

A dream where apostates, some of them close collaborators of God's Messenger, are sent to Hell.

Narrated Abu Huraira:

The Prophet said, "While I was sleeping, a group (of my followers were brought close to me), and when I recognized them, a man (an angel) came out from amongst (us) me and them, he said (to them), 'Come along.'

I asked, 'Where?'

He said, 'To the (Hell) Fire, by Allah.'

I asked, 'What is wrong with them?'

He said, 'They turned apostate as renegades after you left.'

Then behold! (Another) group (of my followers) were brought close to me, and when I recognized them, a man (an angel) came out from (me and them) he said (to them); Come along.'

I asked, 'Where?'

He said, 'To the (Hell) Fire, by Allah.'

I asked, 'What is wrong with them?'

He said, 'They turned apostate as renegades after you left.'

So I did not see anyone of them escaping except a few who were like camels without a shepherd."

Bukhari 76.587

Heaven - The Nuts and Bolts

Excerpt from:

The Islamic Hereafter, Boreal Books

4:57 As to those who have believed and do the good works, We shall admit them into Gardens beneath which rivers flow, abiding therein forever. They have therein purified spouses, and We will admit them to a very shady place.

89:27 O quiescent soul,

89:28 Return unto your Lord well-pleased and well-pleasing;

89:29 And join the ranks of My servants;

89:30 And enter Paradise.

The writing style chosen for this chapter, the chapters *Hell* and *Answering Your Questions about Judgement Day*, which follow, is not meant to be flippant or disrespectful. While the writing style chosen is deliberate, it is not meant to make light of a profoundly serious matter. Quite the opposite! It is meant to show Allah's attention to detail which the believers claim is proof of His existence, the existence of Heaven and Hell and the coming of Judgement Day.

Heaven is just above the clouds and is supported by invisible pillars anchored in the earth (13:2), and that is the truth, but you probably don't believe it.

13:1 Alif – Lam – Mim – Ra.

These are the verses of the Book; and that which has been revealed to you (Muhammad) by your Lord is the truth, but most people do not believe.

13:2 Allah is He Who raised the heavens without pillars that you can see; there He sat upright on the Throne and made the sun and the moon subservient, each running for an appointed term. He manages the [whole] affair and makes clear the Revelations so that you may be certain of meeting your Lord.

31:10 He created the heavens without pillars that you can see and laid down in the earth immovable mountains, lest it shake with you, and scattered throughout it every variety of beast. And We have sent down water from heaven, thereby causing it to grow in it every noble [kind of plant].

31:11 This is Allah's Creation; so show Me what those apart from Him have created. Indeed, the wrongdoers are in manifest error.

Heaven can be compared to a high edifice anchored to a fixed earth.

40:64 It is Allah Who made the earth a fixed station for you and the sky a high edifice. He fashioned you in a shapely manner and provided you with the good things. That for you is Allah, your Lord; so blessed be Allah, the Lord of the Worlds.

Heaven was remodeled into seven levels after Allah created the earth and everything on it.

2:29 It is He Who created for you everything on earth, then ascended to the heavens fashioning them into seven, and He has knowledge of all things.

While busy remodeling Paradise, Allah was not unaware of what He had created below.

23:17 We have created above you seven spheres, and We were not oblivious of the creation.

A much larger heaven is part of Allah's plans.

51:47 And heaven, We have built it mightily, and We shall surely expand it.

Allah's heaven is close by. Neil Armstrong almost made it there. In the Koran, as best as we can discern, heaven or Paradise is just beyond the moon, and the moon is just above the clouds along with the sun which is a large lamp illuminating a flat earth, revelation 78:6.

78:6 Have we not made the earth as a couch for you?

78:7 And the mountains as pegs?

...

78:12 And built above you seven mighty [heavens]?

78:13 And created a shining lamp?

Allah maintains he completed the seven heavens of Paradise in just two days. An accomplishment He is justly proud of. How did He do it?

41:11 Then He arose to heaven while it was smoke, and He said to it and to the earth: "Come over, willingly or unwillingly." They said: "We come willingly."

41:12 Then He completed them as seven heavens in two days and assigned to each heaven its proper order. And We adorned the lower heaven with lamps as protection (from the demons). That is the determination of the All-Mighty, the All-Knowing.

You should be able to see the lowest of the seven levels of Allah's Heaven from the ground.

50:6 Have they not beheld the heaven above them, how We erected it and adorned it, and it has no cracks.

67:1 Blessed be He whose hands is the sovereignty and He has power over everything.

67:2 He Who created death and life so as to test you as to whoever of you is fairer in action. He is the All-Mighty, the All-Forgiving.

67:3 He Who has created seven stratified heavens. You do not see any discrepancy in the creation of the Compassionate. So fix your gaze, do you see any cracks?

Stare too long or too often skyward and you will strain your eyes.

67:4 Then fix your gaze again and again, and your gaze will recoil back to you discomfited and weary.

Some buildings in heaven are made of bricks.

8:32 And when they said: "O Allah, if this is indeed the truth from You, then rain down upon us brickstones from heaven, or inflict upon us a very painful punishment."

The garden (or gardens of Paradise) is one big garden indeed.

57:21 Vie with one another unto forgiveness from your Lord and a Garden the breadth of whereof is like the breadth of the heavens and the earth; it has been prepared for those who believe in Allah and His Messengers. That is Allah's Bounty which He confers upon whoever He pleases. And Allah is the Great Bounty.

Each level of heaven contains two gardens with much greenery, two gushing springs and in addition to fruit trees such as the drought-tolerant pomegranate, trees ordinarily found in oases i.e. palm trees.

55:62 And beneath them (the two gardens) are two other gardens.

55:63 So, which of your Lord's Bounties do you both (Jinn and humans) deny?

55:64 Of dark green colour.

55:65 So, which of your Lord's Bounties do you both (Jinn and humans) deny?

55:66 Therein are two gushing springs.

55:67 So, which of your Lord's Bounties do you both (Jinn and humans) deny?

55:68 Therein are fruits, palm trees and pomegranates.

55:69 So, which of your Lord's Bounties do you both (Jinn and humans) deny?

While Allah does not mention any buildings made of pearl, the Prophet said he saw one there, it is a building for married women only, and it is HUGE.

Allah's Apostle said, "In Paradise there is a pavilion made of a single hollow pearl sixty miles wide, in each corner of which there are wives who will not see those in the other corners; and the believers will visit and enjoy them."

Bukhari 60.402

Most of heaven's buildings may be multi-level (not unlike a modern apartment complex) above a source of fresh water.

39:20 But those who fear their Lord will have chambers over which other chambers are built and beneath which the rivers flow. That is Allah's Promise. Allah does not break His Promise.

A password into Paradise:

41:30 Those who say: "Our Lord is Allah", then are upright, the angels shall descend upon them saying: "Do not fear or grieve, but rejoice in the Paradise which you were promised.

41:31 "We are your protectors in the present life and in the Hereafter, wherein you shall have whatever your hearts desire and you shall have therein whatever you call for;

41:32 "As hospitality from an All-Forgiving, Merciful One."

Appendices

A list of those who will get the equivalent of a penthouse:

> 25:72 Those who do not bear false witness; and when they pass by idle talk, pass by with dignity;

> 25:73 And those who, when reminded of the Sign of their Lord, do not fall down upon them deaf and blind (turn a deaf ear, *Moududi*).

> 25:74 And those who say: "Our Lord, grant us, through our wives and progeny, beloved offsprings, and make us a model for the God fearing."

> 25:75 Those shall be reward with a high chamber (in Paradise) for their steadfastness, and will be received therein with greeting and peace.

> 25:76 Dwelling therein forever. What a delightful resort and lodging!

Single family dwellings are also likely?

> 29:57 Every living soul shall taste death; then unto Us you shall be returned.

> 29:58 Those who have believed and done the righteous deeds, We shall install them in chambers in Paradise, beneath which rivers flow, dwelling therein forever. Blessed is the wage of those who labour!

> 29:59 Those who stood fast and in their Lord they trust.

Some may even have their own palaces.

> 25:10 Blessed is He Who, if He wishes, will accord you better than that – Gardens underneath which rivers flow, and will build palaces for you.

> (Intermediate revelations are in the chapter *Hell*.)

> 25:15 Say: "Is that better (Hell) or the Garden of Eternity which the God-fearing have been promised, as a reward and ultimate resort?"

> 25:16 They have therein what they desire, abiding forever, as a promise binding upon your Lord.

> ----

> 25:24 The companions of Paradise on that Day shall be better lodged and more fairly accommodated.

For some, a piece of land which they call their own:

> 39:73 And those who feared their Lord will be led to Paradise in throngs. Then, when they have reached it and its gates are opened [they will enter it] and its keepers will say; "Peace be upon you; you have fared well, so enter it to dwell therein forever."

> 39:74 They will say: "Praise be to Allah Who has been truthful in His Promise to us and has bequeathed upon us the land wherein we are able to settle in Paradise wherever we wish. Blessed is the wage of the labourers!"

> 39:75 And you will see the angels circling around the Throne proclaiming the praise of their Lord. And it will be justly decided between them and it will be said: "Praise be to Allah, the Lord of the Worlds."

Proper attire will be provided.

> 18:30 As for those who believe and do the good deeds, surely, We will not waste the reward of him who does the good work.

> 18:31 Those shall have Gardens of Eden, beneath which rivers flow, bejeweled therein with bracelets of gold, and wearing green clothes of silk and brocade, reclining therein on couches. Blessed is their reward and fair is the resting place!

Allah has to be enamored with silk to remind the believers at least three more times that He will dress them all in garments made from fibers normally produced by silkworms.

> 22:23 Allah shall admit those who believe and do the righteous deeds into Gardens, beneath which rivers flow. Therein they shall be adorned with gold bracelets and pearls, and their raiment there shall be of silk.

> 22:24 They had been guided to the fair words and guided to the Path of the Praiseworthy.

> ----

> 35:33 Into Gardens of Eden they enter, wherein they are adorned with gold bracelets and pearls and there clothing therein will be silk.

> ----

> 44:51 However, the God-fearing are in a secure place;

> 44:52 In gardens and well-springs.

44:53 They wear silk and brocade facing each other.

Clothing is <u>not</u> optional.

20:118 "You will certainly not be hungry therein, nor be naked.

Sun block will not be required in Heaven.

20:119 "And you will not thirst therein, nor be exposed to the heat of the sun."

Look down and be surprised at who you might see:

37:50 Then, they will advance one towards the other asking each other.

37:51 One of them will say: "I had a comrade;

37:52 "Who used to say: 'Are you then one of the confirmed believers?'

37:53 "Will we, once we are dead and have become dust and bones, be really judged?"

37:54 He said (to his companion): "Are you looking down?"

37:55 He looked and saw him in the centre of Hell.

37:56 He said: "By Allah, you almost caused my perdition.

37:57 "But for my Lord's Grace, I would have been one of those brought forward."

The people of Paradise and the people of Hell will be within shouting distance of each other.

7:44 And the people of Paradise will call out to the people of the Fire: "We have found what our Lord promised us to be true; so have you found what your Lord promised to be true?" They will say: "Yes." Thereupon a caller from their midst shall call out: "May Allah's curse be upon the wrongdoers;

7:45 "Who bar [others] from Allah's Way and desire it to be crooked; and they disbelieve in the Hereafter."

Jesus

Excerpt from:

Shared Prophets, Boreal Books

SINCERITY

112 Al-Ikhlâs

In the Name of Allah,
the Compassionate, the Merciful

112:1 Say: "He is Allah, the only One,

112:2 "Allah, the Everlasting.

112:3 "He did not beget and is not begotten,

112:4 "And none is His equal."

2:116 And they say: "Allah has begotten a son." Glory be to Him. His is everything in the heavens and the earth; all are obedient to Him.

2:117 Creator of the heavens and the earth. When He decrees a thing, He only says to it: "Be," and there it is.

4:171 O People of the Book, do not exceed the bounds of your religion nor say about Allah except the truth. The Messiah, Jesus, son of Mary, is only Allah's Messenger and His Word, which he imparted to Mary, and is a spirit from Him! So believe in Allah and His Messenger and do not say "three" [gods]. Refrain; it is better for you. Allah is truly One God. How – Glory be to Him – could He have a son To him belongs what is in Heaven and on earth? Allah suffices as a Guardian!

4:172 The Messiah does not disdain to be a servant of Allah, nor do the angels nearest to Him ...

10:68 They say: "Allah has taken a child." Glory be to Him! He is the self-sufficient; His is everything in the heavens and on the earth. You have no authority for this. Do you attribute to Allah what you do not know.

The entire concept of the Koran is based on a simple premise: God had gotten fed up with sending his messages on how we should live and how He should be worshipped via prophets who did not communicate His message accurately or were misunderstood by a less than receptive audience. God's patience had run out. He would send one last messenger, his greatest messenger, with his final instructions for mankind: the Koran. Anyone who did not heed the advice of this ultimate messenger was doomed.

There was only one problem with this latest divine plan for getting humanity to behave: *Jesus*. If God had already come down to earth to deliver his message personally in the person of Jesus, then sending another messenger with a final message from God made no sense. If Muhammad's claim to be the last and greatest messenger of God was to have any credibility, the Christian claim that Jesus was the Son of God had to be discredited.

There was also a positive side to Jesus' status. His reputation could also be used to enhance the reputation of an aspiring prophet like the Prophet Muhammad.

Jesus of Nazareth, before the advent of Islam and during the time of the Prophet Muhammad was a much revered figure, even among the pagan tribes of the Arabian Peninsula. It was said that the Prophet's grand-father, Abd al-Muttalib, had prayed to the Christian god to grant him sons, something his pagan gods had proven incapable of doing.

The Prophet Jesus

In many verses Allah will praise the *Prophet Jesus* as a worthy pre-cursor to his greatest prophet. Muslims believe that the "Comforter" promised in the Gospel of St John, chapter 16, verse 7 is the Prophet Muhammad, not Jesus.

> Nevertheless I tell you the truth; it is expedient for me that I go away; for if I go not away; the Comforter will not come onto you; but if I depart, I will send him unto you.

John the Baptist had announced the coming of Jesus; Jesus would announce the coming of the Prophet Muhammad, and who says otherwise is a wrongdoer who wishes to extinguish Allah's Lights.

> 61:6 And when Jesus, son of Mary, said: "O Children of Israel, I am Allah's Messenger to you, confirming what came before me of the Torah, and announcing the news of a Messenger who will come after me, whose name is Ahmad." Then when he (Ahmad i.e. Mohammad) brought them the clear proofs, they said: "This is manifest sorcery."

61:7 And who is a greater wrongdoer than he who imputes falsehoods to Allah, when he is summoned to submission (to Allah)? Allah does not guide the wrongdoing people.

61:8 They wish to extinguish Allah's Lights with their mouths. But Allah will perfect His Light, even though the unbelievers might be averse.

Jesus would even get his disciples to pledge their allegiance to Allah after explaining his mission to them.

3:50 "I have come to confirm what came before me of the Torah and make lawful to you some of the things that were forbidden to you. I have come to you with a sign from your Lord; so fear Allah and obey me."

3:51 "Allah is indeed your Lord and my Lord; so worship Him. This is the straight path!"

3:52 When Jesus sensed their disbelief, he said: "Who are my supporters in Allah's Way?" the disciples said: "We are Allah's supporters; we believe in Allah, so bear witness that we submit."

3:53 "Lord, we believe in what You have revealed, and we have followed the Messenger; write us down with those who bear witness."

61:14 O believers, be supporters of Allah, as Jesus, son of Mary, said to the disciples: "Who are my supporters unto Allah?" The disciples replied: "We are Allah's supporters"; and so a group of the Children of Israel believed, while another group disbelieved. Then, We supported those who believed against their foe; and so they were triumphant.

This negative/positive side to Jesus may explain the apparent schizophrenic nature of many of the verses concerning his person. Unlike when He is praising Jesus the Prophet, whenever Jesus as the Son of God is mentioned in any verse you can almost feel Allah's rage, for example in a revelation as to why He sent the Koran.

18:4 And to warn those who say: "Allah has taken a son."

18:5 They have no knowledge thereof, nor do their fathers. What a dreadful word that comes out of their mouth! They only utter a lie.

An even more vehement denunciation can be found at the end of surah 19, the surah ostensibly dedicated to Mary and which documents most of the events surrounding Jesus' birth. In these revelations Allah is shocked and all His creation appalled by the claim that Jesus is not His servant like everyone else, and like everyone else will appear before Him, by himself, on Judgement Day.

19:88 And they say: "The Compassionate has taken Himself a son,"

19:89 You have indeed made a shocking assertion,

19:90 From which the heavens are almost rent asunder, the earth is split and the mountain fall to pieces.

19:91 For they ascribe a son to the Compassionate.

19:92 Whereas, it is not fitting that the Compassionate should have a son.

19:93 Everyone in the heavens and on earth will surely come to the Compassionate as a servant.

19:94 He keeps count of them and has numbered them.

19:95 And every one of them will come to Him on the Day of Resurrection alone.

The infant Jesus, only a few hours after his birth, at the request of his mother who is being accused of having a child out of wedlock, will loudly proclaim that he is not the Son of God but a prophet sent by Allah, who praises Allah and does as Allah commands.

19:27 Then she brought him (the child) to her people, carrying him. They said: "O Mary, you have surely committed a strange thing.

19:28 "Sister of Aaron, your father was not an evil man and your mother was not unchaste."

19:29 Whereupon she pointed to him. They said: "How will we talk to one who is still an infant in the cradle?"

19:30 He [Jesus] said "Indeed, I am the servant of Allah, Who gave me the Book and made me a Prophet.

19:31 "And He made me blessed wherever I am and has commanded me to pray and to give the alms, so long as I live;

19:32 And be devoted to my mother; and He did not make me arrogant and mischievous.

19:33 "Peace be upon me the day I was born, the day I die and the day I rise from the dead."

In the next verse, Allah echoes the baby Jesus' claim.

19:34 Such was Jesus, son of Mary; it is the truth which they (the Christians) dispute.

Jesus again, boasting about Allah's omnipotence and asking that only Allah be worshipped.

19:35 It is not fitting for Allah to have a son. Glory be to Him; when He decrees a thing, He simply says: "Be", and it comes to be.

19:36 Allah is truly your Lord and my Lord; so worship him. That is a straight path.

Allah again, with how wrong the wrongdoers (those who maintain He has a son) are and how they will be held to account.

19:37 Yet, the sects among them differed. Woe to those who have disbelieved from the spectacle of a great Day!

19:38 How well they will hear and how well they will see, on the Day they will come onto Us; but the wrongdoers today are in manifest error.

19:39 And warn them of the Day of sorrow, when the issue is decided, while they are heedless and do not believe.

Jesus said the meek would inherit the earth. Not so, says Allah.

19:40 It is We Who shall inherit the earth and whomever is on it, and to Us they shall be returned.

Khaibar

Excerpt from:
1,001 Sayings and Deeds of the Prophet Muhammad, Boreal Books

Khaibar is not just another of the many bloody pitiless battles waged by the Prophet Muhammad to establish his rule on the Arabian Peninsula. After Badr, no battle gets more mention in the hadiths than that of Khaibar (also spelled Khaybar). The horde of holy warriors descending on the villages and towns of the Peninsula intent on slaughter, destruction and plunder, with God's Messenger announcing to their inhabitants their imminent annihilation in his god's name, as he does at Khaibar must have been terrifying.

Narrated Anas bin Malik:

Allah's Apostle reached Khaibar in the early morning and the people of Khaibar came out with their spades, and when they saw the Prophet they said, "Muhammad and his army!" and returned hurriedly to take refuge in the fort.

The Prophet raised his hands and said, "Allah is Greater! Khaibar is ruined! If we approach a nation, then miserable is the morning of those who are warned."

Bukhari 56.840

Dawn, in a hadith which says the Prophet reached Kaibar at night, was when the unbelievers could expect the horde's onslaught.

Narrated Anas:

The Prophet set out for Khaibar and reached it at night. He used not to attack if he reached the people at night, till the day broke. So, when the day dawned, the Jews came out with their bags and spades. When they saw the Prophet; they said, "Muhammad and his army!"

The Prophet said, "Allahu Akbar! (Allah is Greater) and Khaibar is ruined, for whenever we approach a nation (i.e. enemy to fight) then it will be a miserable morning for those who have been warned."

Bukhari 52.195

The call to prayer only delayed the inevitable.

Narrated Humaid:

Anas bin Malik said, "Whenever the Prophet went out with us to fight (in Allah's cause) against any nation, he never allowed us to attack till morning and he would wait and see: if he heard Adhan (the call to prayer) he would postpone the attack and if he did not hear Adhan he would attack ..."

Bukhari 11.584

Back to a dawn arrival in a hadith which announces the Prophet's ban on eating the meat of domesticated donkeys.

Narrated Anas:

The Prophet reached Khaibar in the morning, while the people were coming out carrying their spades over their shoulders. When they saw him they said, "This is Muhammad and his army! Muhammad and his army!" So, they took refuge in the fort.

The Prophet raised both his hands and said, "Allahu Akbar, Khaibar is ruined, for when we approach a nation (i.e. enemy to fight) then miserable is the morning of the warned ones."

Then we found some donkeys which we (killed and) cooked. The announcer of the Prophet announced: "Allah and His Apostle forbid you to eat donkey's meat." So, all the pots including their contents were turned upside down.

Bukhari 52.234

You could still however fill your belly with the flesh of the onager, a wild variety of donkey.

Narrated Abu Qatada:

We were in the company of the Prophet at a place called Al-Qaha (which is at a distance of three stages of journey from Medina) ...

I noticed that some of my companions were watching something, so I looked up and saw an onager. (I rode my horse and took the spear and whip) but my whip fell down (and I asked them to pick it up for me) but they said, "We will not help you by any means as we are in a state of Ihram (*sacred state*)." So, I picked up the whip myself and attacked the onager from behind a hillock and slaughtered it and brought it to my companions.

Some of them said, "Eat it." While some others said, "Do not eat it." So, I went to the Prophet who was ahead of us and asked him about it, He replied, "Eat it as it is Halal (i.e. it is legal to eat it)."

Bukhari 29.49

On the day of the battle, the eating of horse flesh was made lawful.

Narrated Jabir bin Abdullah:

On the Day of the battle of Khaibar, Allah's Apostle made donkey's meat unlawful and allowed the eating of horse flesh.

Bukhari 67.429

You should not however spice up your wild donkey or horse meat dish with garlic if you intended to go to mosque before or after the battle.

Narrated Ibn Umar:

During the holy battle of Khaibar the Prophet said, "Whoever ate from this plant (i.e. garlic) should not enter our mosque."

Bukhari 12.812

On the day of the battle temporary marriages were forbidden, or so it would seem.

Narrated Muhammad bin Ali:

Ali was told that Ibn Abbas did not see any harm in the Mut'a marriage. Ali said, "Allah's Apostle forbade the Mut'a marriage on the Day of the battle of Khaibar and he forbade the eating of donkey's meat."

Some people said, "If one, by a tricky way, marries temporarily, his marriage is illegal."

Others said, "The marriage is valid but its condition is illegal."

Bukhari 86.91

The taking of a town or village was as straightforward as it was pitiless: first prayers, then an assault on the unbelievers' position. If successful, as most of these massacres were, then came the plunder and apportioning of the property of the men killed including their wives, daughters and sons which were taken into slavery. Young women and girls were especially prized as slave-girls. At Khaibar, God's Messenger obtained the seventeen year old Safiya (also spelled Safiyya) for his troubles. She would become his eleventh wife.

Narrated Anas bin Malik:

Allah's Apostle (p.b.u.h) offered the Fajr prayer when it was still dark, then he rode and said, "Allah Akbar! Khaibar is ruined. When we approach near to a nation, the most unfortunate is the morning of those who have been warned."

The people came out into the streets saying, "Muhammad and his army."

Allah's Apostle vanquished them by force and their warriors were killed; the children and women were taken as captives. Safiya was taken by Dihya Al-Kalbi and later she belonged to Allah's Apostle who married her and her Mahr (dowry) was her manumission.

Bukhari 14.68

Ali, the Prophet's son-in-law and future Caliph (Leader of the Believers) may have been reluctant to join the fight due to an eye ailment which his father-in-law cured with a dab of saliva.

Narrated Sahl bin Sad:

That he heard the Prophet on the day (of the battle) of Khaibar saying, "I will give the flag to a person at whose hands Allah will grant victory." So, the companions of the Prophet got up, wishing eagerly to see to whom the flag will be given, and every one of them wished to be given the flag. But the Prophet asked for Ali. Someone informed him that he was suffering from eye-trouble. So, he ordered them to bring Ali in front of him.

Then the Prophet spat in his eyes and his eyes were cured immediately as if he had never any eye-trouble.

Ali said, "We will fight with them (i.e. infidels) till they become like us (i.e. Muslims)."

The Prophet said, "Be patient, till you face them and invite them to Islam and inform them of what Allah has enjoined upon them. By Allah! If a single person embraces Islam at your hands (i.e. through you), that will be better for you than the red camels."

Bukhari 52.192

Another account of Ali's lateness in joining the assault on Khaibar:

Narrated Salama bin Al-Akwa:

Ali remained behind the Prophet during the battle of Khaibar as he was suffering from some eye trouble but then he said, "How should I stay behind Allah's Apostle?" So, he set out till he joined the Prophet.

On the eve of the day of the conquest of Khaibar, Allah's Apostle said, "(No doubt) I will give the flag or, tomorrow, a man whom Allah and His Apostle love or who loves Allah and His apostle will take the flag. Allah will bestow victory upon him."

Suddenly Ali joined us though we were not expecting him. The people said, "Here is Ali." So, Allah's Apostle gave the flag to him and Allah bestowed victory upon him.

Bukhari 52.219

During the battle of Khaibar a camel driver and storyteller by the name of Amir apparently committed suicide; but not before dispatching an undetermined number of unbelievers. In the first of two narrations about the circumstances surrounding Amir's demise, it's again donkey meat which gets most of the Prophet's attention.

Narrated Salama bin Al-Akwa':

We went out with the Prophet to Khaibar. A man among the people said, "O Amir! Will you please recite to us some of your poetic verses?" So Amir got down and started chanting among them, saying, "By Allah! Had it not been for Allah, we would not have been guided." Amir also said other poetic verses which I do not remember.

Allah's Apostle said, "Who is this (camel) driver?"

The people said, "He is Amir bin Al-Akwa."

He said, "May Allah bestow His Mercy on him."

A man from the People said, "O Allah's Apostle! Would that you let us enjoy his company longer."

When the people (Muslims) lined up, the battle started, and Amir was struck with his own sword (by chance) by himself and died.

In the evening, the people made a large number of fires (for cooking meals).

Allah's Apostle said, "What is this fire? What are you making the fire for?"

They said, "For cooking the meat of donkeys."

He said, "Throw away what is in the pots and break the pots!"

A man said, "O Allah's Prophet! May we throw away what is in them and wash them?"

He said, "Never mind, you may do so."

Bukhari 75.343

In the second narration, the preoccupation is thankfully no longer about donkey meat but about Amir's death, and whether the way he died – by his own hand or by accident – means that he has voided Allah's guarantee of a reward i.e. Paradise for whomever dies killing unbelievers.

Narrated Salama:

We went out with the Prophet to Khaibar. A man (from the companions) said, "O Amir! Let us hear some of your Huda (camel-driving songs.)" So he sang some of them (i.e. a lyric in harmony with the camels walk).

The Prophet said, "Who is the driver (of these camels)?"

They said, "Amir."

The Prophet said, "May Allah bestow His Mercy on him!"

The people said, "O Allah's Apostle! Would that you let us enjoy his company longer!" Then Amir was killed the following morning.

The people said, "The good deeds of 'Amir are lost as he has killed himself."

I returned at the time while they were talking about that. I went to the Prophet and said, "O Allah's Prophet! Let my father be sacrificed for you! The people claim that Amir's good deeds are lost."

The Prophet said, "Whoever says so is a liar, for Amir will have a double reward as he exerted himself to obey Allah and fought in Allah's Cause. No other way of killing would have granted him greater reward."

Bukhari 83.29

The Prophet Muhammad, as God's Messenger, was not only entitled to one fifth of the booty obtained the hard way, but all the booty that was obtained without a fight, the Fai'. Technically, the valuable farmland surrounding Khaibar had not been fought over therefore under the doctrine of Fai' (see *Booty and the Unbelievers*) it belonged to God's Messenger exclusively.

What made the land around the oasis of Khaibar extraordinarily valuable was the Jewish farmers who worked the land; something the Messenger's holy warriors would not have cared to do, even if they had known how to grow dates and such, for killing and absconding with the belongings of the unbelievers was a much more profitable enterprise. The Prophet let the Jewish farmers of Khaibar continue to work the land in return for half of what they produced.

Narrated Abdullah bin Umar:

Allah's Apostle gave the land of Khaibar to the Jews to work on and cultivate and take half of its yield. Ibn Umar added, "The land used to be rented for a certain portion (of its yield)." Nafi mentioned the amount of the portion but I forgot it.

Rafi bin Khadij said, "The Prophet forbade renting farms."

Narrated Ubaid-Ullah Nafi said: Ibn Umar said: (The contract of Khaibar continued) till Umar evacuated the Jews (from Khaibar).

Bukhari 36.485

Some of the Jewish farmers were not grateful, or simply wanted to test the Prophet's claim to being God's Messenger, therefore under His Protection.

Narrated Abu Huraira:

When Khaibar was conquered, a roasted poisoned sheep was presented to the Prophets as a gift (by the Jews). The Prophet ordered, "Let all the Jews who have been here, be assembled before me."

The Jews were collected and the Prophet said (to them), "I am going to ask you a question. Will you tell the truth?"

They said, "Yes."

The Prophet asked, "Who is your father?"

They replied, "So-and-so."

He said, "You have told a lie; your father is so-and-so."

They said, "You are right."

He said, "Will you now tell me the truth, if I ask you about something?"

They replied, "Yes, O Abu Al-Qasim; and if we should tell a lie, you can realize our lie as you have done regarding our father."

On that he asked, "Who are the people of the (Hell) Fire?"

They said, "We shall remain in the (Hell) Fire for a short period, and after that you will replace us."

The Prophet said, "You may be cursed and humiliated in it! By Allah, we shall never replace you in it."

Then he asked, "Will you now tell me the truth if I ask you a question?"

They said, "Yes, O Abu Al-Qasim."

He asked, "Have you poisoned this sheep?"

They said, "Yes."

He asked, "What made you do so?"

They said, "We wanted to know if you were a liar in which case we would get rid of you, and if you are a prophet then the poison would not harm you."

Bukhari 53.394

The Prophet on his death bed said that the pain he was experiencing was like the ache he felt after eating the poisoned sheep (see chapter *Death of the Prophet - Official Cause*). This saying is largely responsible for the tradition that Jews caused the death of God's Messenger. If they did, this would lend credence to their suspicion that the victor of Khaibar was not who he pretended to be, as unlikely as that may seem.

What the Jewish farmers of Khaibar produced was one of the most profitable acquisitions of the Prophet and may explain his successor's unilateral takeover of God's Messenger's interests.

Narrated Aisha:

Fatima sent somebody to Abu Bakr asking him to give her her inheritance from the Prophet from what Allah had given to His Apostle through Fai (i.e. booty gained without fighting). She asked for the Sadaqa (i.e. wealth assigned for charitable purposes) of the Prophet at Medina, and Fadak, and what remained of the Khumus (i.e., one-fifth) of the Khaibar booty.

Abu Bakr said, "Allah's Apostle said, 'We (Prophets), our property is not inherited, and whatever we leave is Sadaqa, but Muhammad's Family can eat from this property, i.e. Allah's property, but they have no right to take more than the food they need.' By Allah! I will not bring any change in dealing with the Sadaqa of the Prophet (and will keep them) as they used to be observed in his (i.e. the Prophet's) life-time, and I will dispose with it as Allah's Apostle used to do,"

Then Ali said, "I testify that None has the right to be worshipped but Allah, and that Muhammad is His Apostle," and added, "O Abu Bakr! We acknowledge your superiority." Then he (i.e. Ali) mentioned their own relationship to Allah's Apostle and their right.

Abu Bakr then spoke saying, "By Allah in Whose Hands my life is. I love to do good to the relatives of Allah's Apostle rather than to my own relatives"

Abu Bakr added: Look at Muhammad through his family (i.e. if you are not good to his family you are not good to him).

Bukhari 57.60

Fatima the Prophet's daughter and mother of his grandsons confronted Bakr, but was unsuccessful in getting him to give her what should have been her due. Bakr's excuse was that he needed her father's legacy for charitable works and to feed his now destitute widows who were also denied a share of their husband's estate.

Narrated Aisha:

Fatima and Al Abbas came to Abu Bakr, seeking their share from the property of Allah's Apostle and at that time, they were asking for their land at Fadak and their share from Khaibar.

Abu Bakr said to them, "I have heard from Allah's Apostle saying, 'Our property cannot be inherited, and whatever we leave is to be spent in charity, but the family of Muhammad may take their provisions from this property."

Abu Bakr added, "By Allah, I will not leave the procedure I saw Allah's Apostle following during his lifetime concerning this property." Therefore Fatima left Abu Bakr and did not speak to him till she died.

Bukhari 80.718

Bakr, by absconding with the Prophet's estate and Allah by forbidding any man to marry His Messenger's wives after his passing (33:53 ... You should never hurt the Messenger of Allah, nor take his wives in marriage after him ...), meant that they were reduced to the status of beggars, dependent on the whims of the parsimonious acquisitive Bakr for their survival.

Umar would eventually expel all Jews and Christians from the Hejaz, the so-called holy land of Islam centered on Mecca and Medina, which comprises most of the western part of modern-day Saudi Arabia.

Narrated Ibn Umar:

Umar bin Al-Khattab expelled all the Jews and Christians from the land of Hijaz. Allah's Apostle after conquering Khaibar, thought of expelling the Jews from the land which, after he conquered it belonged to Allah, Allah's Apostle and the Muslims. But the Jews requested Allah's Apostle to leave them there on the condition that they would do the labor and get half of the fruits (the land would yield).

Allah's Apostle said, "We shall keep you on these terms as long as we wish." Thus they stayed till the time of Umar's Caliphate when he expelled them to Taima and Ariha.

Bukhari 53.380

Umar accused the Jews of harming a believer, then used what the Jews thought was a joke made at their expense by the Prophet (Abu-l-Qasim in the following hadith) to nullify God's Messenger's agreement.

Narrated Ibn Umar:

When the people of Khaibar dislocated Abdullah bin Umar's hands and feet, Umar got up delivering a sermon saying, "No doubt, Allah's Apostle made a contract with the Jews concerning their properties, and said to them, 'We allow you (to stand in your land) as long as Allah allows you.' Now Abdullah bin Umar went to his land and was attacked at night, and his hands and feet were dislocated, and as we have no enemies there except those Jews, they are our enemies and the only people whom we suspect, I have made up my mind to exile them."

When Umar decided to carry out his decision, a son of Abu Al-Haqiq's came and addressed Umar, "O chief of the believers, will you exile us although Muhammad allowed us to stay at our places, and made a contract with us about our properties, and accepted the condition of our residence in our land?"

Umar said, "Do you think that I have forgotten the statement of Allah's Apostle: 'What will your condition be when you are expelled from Khaibar and your camel will be carrying you night after night?'"

The Jew replied, "That was a joke from Abu-l-Qasim."

Umar said, "O the enemy of Allah! You are telling a lie."

Umar then drove them out and paid them the price of their properties in the form of fruits, money, camel saddles and ropes, etc.

Bukhari 50.890

Umar, Bakr's successor would return some of the Prophet's property which was allegedly meant for charity to Ali, Fatima's husband. The property had probably lost much of its value after Umar exiled the Jews who farmed the land.

Massacre of the Banu Qurayzah

Excerpt from:
Allah's War Against the Unbelievers, Boreal Books

With Medina secure for the time being, the Prophet received an order from the angel Gabriel to attack the Banu Qurayzah whose leaders are said to have plotted with the Meccans during the Battle of the Ditch.

Narrated Aisha:

When Allah's Apostle returned on the day (of the battle) of Al-Khandaq (i.e. Trench), he put down his arms and took a bath. Then Gabriel whose head was covered with dust, came to him saying, "You have put down your arms! By Allah, I have not put down my arms yet."

Allah's Apostle said, "Where (to go now)?"

Gabriel said, "This way," pointing towards the tribe of Bani Quraiza. So Allah's Apostle went out towards them.

Bukhari 52.68

He marched on their fortress just outside Medina with three thousand jihadists. When he neared the fortress he called out to its defenders: "O brothers of monkeys and pigs! Fear me, fear me." The simian reference would make its way into the Koran as a persistent reminder of the perfidy of the Jews and an incitement for future generations of the righteous.

2:65 And you surely know those of you who violated the Sabbath; We said to them: "Be [like] dejected apes."

2:66 Thus We made an example to their contemporaries and to those after them, and admonition to the righteous.

Another revelation in the same vein:

7:166 Then, when they disdained arrogantly what they were forbidden, We said to them: "Be miserable monkeys."

After twenty five days, the Banu Qurayzah asked for a mediator. The Prophet sent Abu Lubabah who matter-of-factly informed the Jews that the Prophet had slaughter on his mind.

When they saw him (Lubabah), the men rose to meet him, and the women and children rushed to grab hold of him, weeping before him, so that he felt pity for them. They said to him, "Abu Lubabah, do you think that we should submit to Muhammad's judgment?"

"Yes", he said, but he pointed with his hand to his throat, that it would be slaughter.

Tabari

The Banu Qurayzah asked the Prophet to be allowed to go into exile. God's Messenger rejected their proposal and insisted that they submit themselves to his judgment. Abu Lubabah would not be a witness to the result of his negotiations with the Jews. It was probably just as well.

Abu Lubabah felt guilty that he had broken his promise of secrecy with Muhammad. To atone for his 'misdeed' he went straight to the mosque and bound himself with ropes to one of the pillars. This pillar is known as the 'pillar of repentance' or the 'pillars of Abu Lubabah'.

Abul Kasem

Lubabah spent six days chained to his pillar. He was freed by the Prophet after God's Messenger received the following revelation.

8:27 O you who believe, do not betray Allah and the Messenger, nor betray your trust knowingly.

Ignoring Lubabah's warning, the Banu Qurayzah surrendered en-masse to the Prophet. They agreed to a proposal by God's Messenger that a mortally wounded believer by the name of Sad bin Mu'adh decide their fate.

Some people (the Banu Qurayzah) agreed to accept the verdict of Sad bin Mu'adh so the Prophet sent for him. He came riding a donkey, and when he approached the Mosque, the Prophet said, "Get up for the best amongst you." or said, "Get up for your chief."

Then the Prophet said, "O Sad! These people have agreed to accept your verdict."

Sad said, "I judge that their warriors should be killed and their children and women should be taken as captives."

The Prophet said, "You have given a judgment similar to Allah's Judgment."

Bukhari, 58.148

Appendices

A trench was dug in Medina's marketplace and the estimated seven-hundred male and teenaged boys of the Banu Qurayzah were beheaded with the Prophet of Mercy looking on.

> ...the messenger of God commanded that furrows should be dug in the ground for the B. Qurayzah. Then he sat down, and Ali and al-Zubayr began cutting off their heads in his presence.
>
> *Tabari*

> The messenger of God went out into the marketplace of Medina and had trenches dug in it; then he sent for them and had them beheaded in those trenches. They were brought out to him in groups ... They numbered 600 or 700—the largest estimate says they were between 800 and 900 ... the affair continued until the Messenger of God had finished with them.
>
> *Tabari*

One woman was also beheaded that day. During the siege of the fortress of the Banu Qurayzah she had killed a Muslim soldier by dropping a millstone on his head. Her death as narrated by the Prophet's child bride Aisha.

> Only one of their women was killed. By God, she was by me, talking with me and laughing unrestrainedly while the Messenger of God was killing their men in the marketplace, when suddenly a mysterious voice called out her name, saying, "Where is so and so?"
>
> She said, "I shall be killed."
>
> "Why?" I asked.
>
> She said, "a misdeed that I committed."
>
> She was taken away and beheaded.'

God's Messenger had ordered that all Jewish males with pubic hair were to be killed; but he did spare one boy who took refuge with a Muslim woman who pleaded with the Prophet to spare the boy's life. Her pleading for mercy may not have been necessary if the following story as told by the boy in question is accurate.

> I was among the captives of Banu Qurayzah. They examined us, and those who had begun to grow hair (pubes) were killed, and those who had not were not killed. I was among those who had not grown hair.
>
> *Abu Dawud*

The dead men's wives and daughters were sold into slavery, except for the beautiful widow Rayhanah which God's Messenger made his concubine. Rayhanah turned down the Prophet's marriage proposal thinking it unseemly considering the recent mass murder of the male members of her tribe.

Sad bin Mu'adh also died that day. The Prophet said that Allah's throne shook when he died, so moved was the Almighty by the death of a man who had the courage to cold-bloodily send His enemies to their death and their wives and daughters into slavery.

It should not come as a surprise that Allah was all shook up when he greeted Sad bin Mu'adh in Paradise; after all, not only did He approve of Sad bin Mu'adh's decision but it was His terrorizing of the Jews which drove them to seek mercy from His Messenger with His knowing full well that none was forthcoming.

> 33:26 And He brought those of the People of the Book who supported them from their fortresses and cast terror into their hearts, some of them you slew and some you took captive.

Not to be overlooked was the property of the deceased i.e. the booty which provided Allah, and still does, with the means of rewarding the willing executioners of His alleged enemies.

> 33:27 And He bequeathed to you their lands, their homes and their possessions, together with land you have never trodden. Allah has power over everything.

News of the massacre spread throughout the Arabian Peninsula and not unlike the massacres committed by those who follow the example of the Prophet today inspired both fear and admiration. One thing the massacre made perfectly clear is that you had to choose a side; you could not remain neutral in the war between the believers and unbelievers of which the Arab civil war was the opening gambit. You either chose to become a Muslim and agreed to fight and kill to establish Allah's Kingdom on earth or you became a target of the believers, to be hunted down and slaughtered.

Many converted to Islam after the massacre, not only because they believed that a man who would do such a thing could not be stopped, but to join in the general pillage of the unbelievers' property. All you had to say was "I declare there is no god except God, and I declare that Muhammad is the Messenger of God" and you could with impunity kill or enslave those who refused to say those magic life-saving words and help yourself to their property, their wives and their daughters for your troubles, and still be guaranteed a place in Paradise.

Stoning

Excerpt from:

1,001 Sayings and Deeds of the Prophet Muhammad, Boreal Books

Narrated Abdullah:

I or somebody, asked Allah's Apostle "Which is the biggest sin in the Sight of Allah?"

He said, "That you set up a rival (in worship) to Allah though He Alone created you."

I asked, "What is next?"

He said, "Then, that you kill your son, being afraid that he may share your meals with you."

I asked, "What is next?"

He said, "That you commit illegal sexual intercourse with the wife of your neighbor."

Then the following Verse was revealed to confirm the statement of Allah's Apostle: "Those who invoke not with Allah, any other god, nor kill life as Allah has forbidden except for just cause, nor commit illegal sexual intercourse." (25:68)

Bukhari 60.284

The Prophet said that having illegal intercourse is the third worst sin you can commit. From a woman's point of view, it may be the first. The first two you can ask forgiveness and do it right and all is forgiven; but a woman who has had illegal sex is doomed.

Alice: Adultery is not a sin against Allah or His Messenger, so why is an adulteress not deserving of Allah's Mercy?

Imam: Because there is no way for a woman to make amends for having had sex with someone other than her husband. How would you undo that? How could she undo the dishonour that she has brought on herself, her family and her husband? It is not enough that the adulteress will roast in Hell for eternity, but steps must be taken in the here-and-now to eradicate the reminder of this dishonour and to discourage such destructive behavior.

Alice: Such as stoning the adulteress to death.

From the one act play *Alice visits a Mosque to learn about Judgement Day*, Boreal Books, 2013

It is definitely not a laughing matter:

> [The Prophet] said, "O community of Muhammad! By Allah, there is no-one more jealous than Allah of a male or female slave of his who commits adultery. O community of Muhammad! By Allah, if you knew what I knew, you would laugh little and weep much."

Malik's Muwatta 12.12.1.1

God's Messenger acquired the unlikely moniker *Prophet of Mercy* after the fall of Mecca when he publically spared the lives of some of his opponents while quietly having those with no protectors assassinated e.g. poets and apostates. Other vulnerable human beings for whom the Prophet of Mercy had no compassion were women and girls who committed *illegal intercourse*, even when the less than self-evident crime resulted in a pregnancy. One of the more wretched decisions of the Prophet of Mercy:

> Malik related to me from Yaqub ibn Zayd ibn Talha from his father Zayd ibn Talha that Abdullah ibn Abi Mulayka informed him that a woman came to the Messenger of Allah, may Allah bless him and grant him peace, and informed him that she had committed adultery and was pregnant.
>
> The Messenger of Allah, may Allah bless him and grant him peace, said to her, "Go away until you give birth."
>
> When she had given birth, she came to him. The Messenger of Allah, may Allah bless him and grant him peace, said to her, "Go away until you have suckled and weaned the baby."
>
> When she had weaned the baby, she came to him. He said, "Go and entrust the baby to someone."
>
> She entrusted the baby to someone and then came to him. He gave the order and she was stoned.

Malik's Muwatta 41.41.1.5

That the Prophet of Mercy did not have unwed mothers horribly put to death until they had given birth and weaned their newborn is proof that, at least, the man revered as the embodiment of the perfect human being whose every action must be emulated as closely as possible, cared about babies born out of wedlock; but not enough to not deprive them of their mothers after only two short years.

2:233 Mothers shall suckle their children for two whole years ...

In another hadith about a defenceless woman being put to death on orders from God's Messenger, the Prophet of Mercy simply sent a trusted assassin to enquire from a woman if she had committed adultery and if she answered in the affirmative, to stone her.

Narrated Zaid bin Khalid and Abu Huraira:

The Prophet said, "O Unais! Go to the wife of this (man) and if she confesses (that she has committed illegal sexual intercourse), then stone her to death."

Bukhari 38.508

A more complete account of why this unfortunate woman had to die.

Narrated Abu Huraira and Zaid bin Khalid Al-Juhani:

A bedouin came to Allah's Apostle and said, "O Allah's apostle! I ask you by Allah to judge my case according to Allah's Laws."

His opponent, who was more learned than he, said, "Yes, judge between us according to Allah's Laws, and allow me to speak."

Allah's Apostle said, "Speak."

He (i .e. the bedouin or the other man) said, "My son was working as a laborer for this (man) and he committed illegal sexual intercourse with his wife. The people told me that it was obligatory that my son should be stoned to death, so in lieu of that I ransomed my son by paying one hundred sheep and a slave girl. Then I asked the religious scholars about it, and they informed me that my son must be lashed one hundred lashes, and be exiled for one year, and the wife of this (man) must be stoned to death."

Allah's Apostle said, "By Him in Whose Hands my soul is, I will judge between you according to Allah's Laws. The slave-girl and the sheep are to be returned to you, your son is to receive a hundred lashes and be exiled for one year. You, Unais, go to the wife of this (man) and if she confesses her guilt, stone her to death."

Unais went to that woman next morning and she confessed. Allah's Apostle ordered that she be stoned to death.

Bukhari 50.885

In one recollection of an unlikely stoning of a man, the Prophet conducts an extensive, explicit interrogation in which he tries to save the man from himself (I doubt very much that if the person appearing before him had been a female, God's Messenger would have encouraged her, as he does a man in the following hadith, to confess to a lesser crime).

The chagrin God's Messenger experiences in having to sentence a man to be stoned to death is very much evident in his demand that the people who said he had died like a dog eat from the decaying corpse of an ass. That chagrin may be somewhat diminished by the knowledge that stoning a person to death for adultery, while it has no salutary effect on a female, absolves a male of his sin, and Paradise is within reach.

Narrated AbuHurayrah:

A man of the tribe of Aslam came to the Prophet (peace be upon him) and testified four times against himself that he had had illicit intercourse with a woman, while all the time the Prophet (peace be upon him) was turning away from him. Then when he confessed a fifth time, he turned round and asked: Did you have intercourse with her?

He replied: Yes.

He asked: Have you done it so that your sexual organ penetrated hers?

He replied: Yes.

He asked: Have you done it like a collyrium stick when enclosed in its case and a rope in a well?

He replied: Yes.

He asked: Do you know what fornication is?

He replied: Yes. I have done with her unlawfully what a man may lawfully do with his wife.

He then asked: What do you want from what you have said?

He said: I want you to purify me.

So he gave orders regarding him and he was stoned to death. Then the Prophet (peace be upon him) heard one of his companions saying to another: Look at this man whose fault was concealed by Allah but who would not leave the matter alone, so that he was stoned like a dog.

He said nothing to them but walked on for a time till he came to the corpse of an ass with its legs in the air. He asked: Where are so and so?

They said: Here we are, Apostle of Allah (peace be upon him)!

He said: Go down and eat some of this ass's corpse.

They replied: Apostle of Allah! Who can eat any of this?

He said: The dishonour you have just shown to your brother is more serious than eating some of it. By Him in Whose hand my soul is, he is now among the rivers of Paradise and plunging into them.

Abu Dawud 38.4414

One last hadith about a man who would not take a hint:

Narrated Ibn Abbas:

When Ma'iz bin Malik came to the Prophet (in order to confess), the Prophet said to him, "Probably you have only kissed (the lady), or winked, or looked at her?"

He said, "No, O Allah's Apostle!"

The Prophet said, using no euphemism, "Did you have sexual intercourse with her?"

The narrator added: At that, (i.e. after his confession) the Prophet ordered that he be stoned (to death).

Bukhari 82.813

Whip her, whip her good and whip her again. Slave girls got a break from the Prophet of Mercy:

Narrated Abu Huraira and Said bin Khalid:

The verdict of Allah's Apostle was sought about an unmarried slave girl guilty of illegal intercourse.

He replied, "If she commits illegal sexual intercourse, then flog her (fifty stripes), and if she commits illegal sexual intercourse (after that for the second time), then flog her (fifty stripes), and if she commits illegal sexual intercourse (for the third time), then flog her (fifty stripes) and sell her for even a hair rope."

Ibn Shihab said, "I am not sure whether the Prophet ordered that she be sold after the third or fourth time of committing illegal intercourse."

Bukhari 82.822

The Prophet appears to make a distinction between slave girls having sex outside the sanctity of marriage and females taken as booty which were routinely raped with the Prophet's approval, as long as the rapist avoids coitus interruptus.

Abu Sirma said to Abu Sa'id al Khadri (Allah be pleased with him):

0 Abu Sa'id, did you hear Allah's Messenger (may peace be upon him) mentioning al-'azl?

He said: Yes, and added: We went out with Allah's Messenger (may peace be upon him) on the expedition to the Bi'l- Mustaliq and took captive some excellent Arab women; and we desired them, for we were suffering from the absence of our wives, (but at the same time) we also desired ransom for them.

So we decided to have sexual intercourse with them but by observing 'azl (withdrawing the male sexual organ before emission of semen to avoid conception).

But we said: We are doing an act whereas Allah's Messenger is amongst us; why not ask him?

So we asked Allah's Messenger (may peace be upon him), and he said: It does not matter if you do not do it, for every soul that is to be born up to the Day of Resurrection will be born.

Imam Muslim 8:3371

The Prophet's fondness for stoning those who committed illegal intercourse was undoubtedly influenced by the punishment specified in the Torah.

Narrated Abdullah bin Umar:

The Jews came to Allah's Apostle and told him that a man and a woman from amongst them had committed illegal sexual intercourse.

Allah's Apostle said to them, "What do you find in the Torah (old Testament) about the legal punishment of Ar-Rajm (stoning)?"

They replied, (But) we announce their crime and lash them."

Abdullah bin Salam said, "You are telling a lie; Torah contains the order of Rajm."

They brought and opened the Torah and one of them solaced his hand on the Verse of Rajm and read the verses preceding and following it.

Abdullah bin Salam said to him, "Lift your hand."

When he lifted his hand, the Verse of Rajm was written there. They said, "Muhammad has told the truth; the Torah has the Verse of Rajm."

The Prophet then gave the order that both of them should be stoned to death.

(Abdullah bin Umar said, "I saw the man leaning over the woman to shelter her from the stones."

Bukhari 56.829

God's Messenger boasted that through him Allah would eliminate adultery. This may also explain his pitiless rulings, especially where women accused of adultery were concerned.

Narrated Jubair bin Mutim:

Allah's Apostle said, "I have five names: I am Muhammad and Ahmad; I am Al-Mahi through whom Allah will eliminate infidelity; I am Al-Hashir who will be the first to be resurrected, the people being resurrected there after; and I am also Al-'Aqib (i.e. There will be no prophet after me)."

Bukhari 56.732

Today you never hear of a man getting stoned for illegal intercourse, it is always women and girls, and here's why, according to Syed Shahabuddin writing in the Milli Gazette, Indian Muslim's leading English newspaper:

Apart from the brutality of the 'Rajm' (stoning), repugnant to conscience, here is an element of gender injustice in the operation of the traditional law which allows the male partner to get off scot-free, even if he has coerced and raped the female. If the woman lodges a complaint, her complaint is taken as a testimony against herself and, therefore, amounts to admission and requires no further evidence while it is necessary to get 4 witnesses against the man. Also the woman may bear a child, as in Amina's case (Amina Lawal was sentenced to death by stoning by a Nigerian Islamic Sharia Court. Amina had an 8 month old daughter), which is admitted as evidence of zena (guilt) against the woman. Man suffers from no such disability.

If the slaves of Allah, women mostly, are stoned to death for illegal intercourse it is not their fault, really, it all has to do with Allah's self-respect.

Narrated Aisha:

In the life-time of Allah's Apostle (p.b.u.h) the sun eclipsed, so he led the people in prayer, and stood up and performed a long Qiyam, then bowed for a long while. He stood up again and performed a long Qiyam but this time the period of standing was shorter than the first.

He bowed again for a long time but shorter than the first one, then he prostrated and prolonged the prostration. He did the same in the second Raka as he did in the first and then finished the prayer; by then the sun (eclipse) had cleared.

He delivered the Khutba (sermon) and after praising and glorifying Allah he said, "The sun and the moon are two signs against the signs of Allah; they do not eclipse on the death or life of anyone. So when you see the eclipse, remember Allah and say Takbir, pray and give Sadaqa."

The Prophet then said, "O followers of Muhammad! By Allah! There is none who has more Ghira (self-respect) than Allah as He has forbidden that His slaves, male or female commit adultery (illegal sexual intercourse). O followers of Muhammad! By Allah! If you knew that which I know you would laugh little and weep much."

Bukhari 17.154

Male competition as to who has the greatest self-respect, a self-respect that comes closest to the Ghira of Allah may have a lot to do with so-called honour killings.

Narrated Al-Mughira:

Sa'd bin Ubada said, "If I saw a man with my wife, I would strike him (behead him) with the blade of my sword."

This news reached Allah's Apostle who then said, "You people are astonished at Sa'd's Ghira. By Allah, I have more Ghira than he, and Allah has more Ghira than I, and because of Allah's Ghira, He has made unlawful Shameful deeds and sins (illegal sexual intercourse etc.) done in open and in secret. And there is none who likes that the people should repent to Him and beg His pardon than Allah, and for this reason He sent the warners and the givers of good news. And there is none who likes to be praised more than Allah does, and for this reason, Allah promised to grant Paradise (to the doers of good)."

Abdul Malik said, "No person has more Ghira than Allah."

Bukhari 93.512

If only the Prophet had shown the same disgust at launching rocks at a woman's head until she died as he did at throwing stones at animals.

Narrated Abdullah bin Mughaffal Al-Muzani:

The Prophet forbade the throwing of stones (with the thumb and the index or middle finger), and said "It neither hunts a game nor kills (or hurts) an enemy, but it gouges out an eye or breaks a tooth."

Bukhari 73.239

The Stoning Ritual

Amina would have been placed in a cloth sack with her hands tied behind her back and buried in the ground up to her shoulders. She is not buried up to her neck allegedly to allow her to wriggle free and prove her innocence before a missile hits its mark, and not to make the whole thing more sporting for the men who will be hurling stones at her head while chanting "Allah hu Akbar" (God is great). On October 27, 2008 13-year-old Aisha Ibrahim Duhulow was killed in this manner in a stadium in the southern port of Kismayu, Somalia in front of an estimated 1,000 spectators.

Why you still have these atrocities committed to this day:

Narrated Ibn Abbas:

Umar said, "I am afraid that after a long time has passed, people may say, "We do not find the Verses of the Rajam (stoning to death) in the Holy Book," and consequently they may go astray by leaving an obligation that Allah has revealed. Lo! I confirm that the penalty of Rajam be inflicted on him who commits illegal sexual intercourse, if he is already married and the crime is proved by witnesses or pregnancy or confession."

Sufyan added, "I have memorized this narration in this way."

Umar added, "Surely Allah's Apostle carried out the penalty of Rajam, and so did we after him."

Bukhari 82.816.

Tabuk

Excerpt from:

Allah's War Against the Unbelievers, Boreal Books

9:38 O Believers, what is the matter with you? If you are told: "March forth in the Way of Allah", you simply cling heavily to the ground. Are you satisfied with the present life rather than the Hereafter? Yet the pleasures of the present life are very small compared with those of the Hereafter.

9:39 If you do not march forth, He will inflict a very painful punishment on you and replace you by another people, and you will not harm him (the Prophet) in the least; for Allah has power over everything.

9:41 Charge forth, on foot or mounted, and struggle with your possessions and yourselves in the Way of Allah. That is far better for you, if only you knew.

The Prophet gave credence to his plans to take his battle to the unbelievers far and wide with an expedition to Tabuk in northwestern Saudi Arabia, then part of the Byzantine Empire.

He assembled an army of more than 30 thousand and marched north 889 kms (552 miles) intending to engage the Byzantine forces at Tabuk. The Byzantine did not show up. The lesson was not lost on the locals, not only Arabs but many Christians who flocked to the Prophet's banner. When the Muslims returned there would be no stopping them.

The expedition to Tabuk was one battle too far for many of the believers. They asked to stay behind and, to Allah's initial dismay, the Prophet agreed. Allah had choice words for His Messenger and questioned the allegiance of many of those who sought to avoid the long journey north.

9:42 Had it been a gain near at hand and a short journey, they surely would have followed you. But the distance seemed too long to them. Still they will swear by Allah: "Had we been able, we would have marched forth with you." They damn themselves, and Allah knows that they are liars.

9:43 May Allah pardon you! Why did you allow them [to stay behind] before it became clear to you who were the truthful ones, and you knew who were the liars?

9:44 Those who believe in Allah and the Last Day do not ask you for [exemption from] fighting in the Way of Allah with their wealth and lives. Allah knows well the righteous.

9:45 Only those who do not believe in Allah and the Last Day will ask you [for exemption] and their hearts are in doubt. Thus they vacillate in their state of doubt.

Allah then changes His tune, as He often does in these situations, and explains that it was all His doing if some of them were reluctant to join the Prophet on his expedition to the southern frontier of the Byzantine Empire.

9:46 Had they wanted to go forth, they would have made preparations for that; but Allah was averse to their going forth, and so He held them back, and it was said to them: "Sit back with those who sit back."

9:47 Had they gone out with you, they would have only increased your confusion, and would have kept moving among you sowing sedition. And some of you would have listened to them. Allah knows well the wrongdoers.

9:48 They have sought to sow sedition before and turned things around for you, until the truth came out and Allah's Command was manifested, although they were averse [to it].

9:49 Some of them say: "Allow me and do not tempt me." Indeed they have already fallen into temptation and Hell shall encompass the unbelievers.

9:50 If a good fortune befalls you, they are displeased, and if a disaster befalls you they say: "We took our precautions before." Then, they turn away rejoicing.

9:51 Say: "Nothing will befall us except what Allah has decreed for us. He is our Lord, and in Allah let the believers put their trust.

Allah tells His Messenger to remind those who wish to stay behind that he, the Prophet, is also His instrument for meting out punishment.

9:52 Say: "Do you expect for us anything other than one of the two fairest outcome (martyrdom or victory); while we await for you that Allah will smite you with a punishment, either from Himself, or at our hands?" So wait and watch, we are waiting and watching with you.

Some offered money to get an exemption against this Jihad against the Byzantines.

9:53 Say: "Spend willingly or unwillingly; it shall not be accepted from you. You are truly a sinful people."

9:54 And nothing prevents what they spend from being accepted but that they disbelieve in Allah and His Messenger and that they do not perform the prayer except lazily, and do not spend [anything] except grudgingly.

The Prophet may have granted exemptions to fathers who did not want to be away from their children for months on end. This did not sit well with Allah, Who explained that even children were part of His Plan, therefore, not a valid reason to be exempted from the fighting, no matter how far.

9:55 So do not let their wealth and their children win your approval, Allah only wishes to torture them therewith in the present life, so that their souls might depart while they are still unbelievers.

Why some did not care to accompany God's Messenger on a long journey:

9:56 They swear by Allah that they [are believers] like you, but they are not; they are a people who fear you.

9:57 If they could find a shelter or dens or any place to crawl into, they would make for it in a great haste.

It was during the return trip from Tabuk that the Prophet got wind of an alleged assassination plot which led to some foreboding revelations about unbelievers and hypocrites.

9:73 O Prophet, fight the unbelievers and the hypocrites and be stern with them. Their abode is Hell, and what a terrible fate!

9:74 They swear by Allah that they said nothing [evil], but they said the word of disbelief and disbelieved after professing Islam, and they aimed at (according to some commentators they aimed at killing the Prophet while he was returning from Tabuk) what they could not attain. They only resented that Allah and His Messenger have enriched them from His Bounty. If they repent, it will be better for them; but if they turn away, Allah will inflict a very painful punishment on them in this world and the Hereafter, and they will have on earth no friend or supporter.

9:75 And some of them make a compact with Allah: "If He give us of His Bounty, we shall give in charity and be among the righteous."

9:76 But when He gave them of His Bounty, they grew mean and turned away disobediently.

9:77 So He caused hypocrisy to cling to their hearts until the day they meet Him, on account of revoking what they promised Allah and on account of lying.

9:78 Do they not know that Allah knows their hidden thoughts and private talk, and that Allah knows fully the things unseen?

9:79 Those disparage the believers who give voluntary alms and those find nothing to offer but their outmost endeavour, and they scoff at them. May Allah mock them. There is a painful punishment [in store] for them.

9:80 Ask forgiveness for them or do not ask forgiveness for them. If you ask forgiveness for them seventy times, Allah will not forgive them; because they disbelieve in Allah and His Messenger. Allah does not guide the sinful people.

Some may have stayed behind because they were worried about the heat.

9:81 Those who stayed behind rejoiced at tarrying behind the Messenger of Allah and hated to struggle with their wealth and their lives in Allah's Path, saying: "Do not march forth in the heat." Say: "The Fire of Hell is hotter, if only they could understand."

9:82 Let them laugh a little and cry a lot, as a reward for what they used to do.

While Allah waited to burn those who stayed behind in Hell, His Messenger was not allowed to have them join him on further expeditions.

9:83 Then, if Allah brings you back to a party of them and they ask your permission to go forth with you, say: "You will never go forth with me, and you will never fight with me against any enemy. You were content to sit back the first time; so sit back with those who stay behind."

As to attending their funeral, don't bother:

9:84 And do not ever pray over any one of them who dies, or be present at their grave; indeed they disbelieve in Allah and His Messenger, and died still ungodly.

Again with the children and the wealth:

9:85 And do not let their wealth or children win your admiration. Allah only wishes to punish them therewith in the present life, so that their souls might depart while they are still unbelievers.

Perhaps the ultimate insult, revelation 9:87:

9:86 And if a Surah is revealed stating: "Believe in Allah and fight along with His Messenger", the affluent among them will ask your permission and say: "Let us be with those who stay behind."

9:87 They are content to be among the women who stay behind, and a seal is set upon their hearts, and thus they do not understand.

What those who went to Tabuk can expect:

9:88 But the Messenger and those who believe with him struggle with their wealth and their lives. To those are the good things reserved, and those are the prosperous.

9:89 Allah has prepared for them Gardens beneath which rivers flow, abiding therein forever. That is the great triumph!

Even the desert Arabs i.e. bedouins don't escape Allah's criticism.

9:90 Some of the desert Arabs who gave excuses came to seek permission, whereas those who lied to Allah and His Messenger stayed behind. Those of them who disbelieved shall be afflicted with a very painful punishment.

Allah did allow for some exceptions for the weak and the sick and for those who could not afford to make the journey to Tabuk, and those for whom transportation was not available.

9:91 The weak, the sick, and those who have nothing to spend are not at fault, if they are true to Allah and His Messenger. There can be no blame on the beneficent; and Allah is All-Forgiving, Merciful.

9:92 Nor on those who, when they came to you for mounts asking you for mounts, you said: "I do not find that whereon I can mount you." Thereupon they went back, their eyes overflowing with tears, sorrowing for not finding the means to spend (to provide the expenses of war).

As often happens during these long rants, Allah repeats himself, perhaps for effect.

9:93 The blame is on those who ask your permission, although they are rich. They are content to join those women who stay behind. Allah has placed a seal upon their hearts and so they do not know.

More revelations about the people the Prophet allowed to stay behind, supposedly received on the return journey, prompting another round of questioning when God's Messenger reached Medina.

9:94 They present to you [false] excuses when you return to them. Say: "Do not offer excuses; we will not believe you. Allah has told us [all] about you. Allah shall see your work, and His Messenger too. Then you will be turned over to Him Who knows the unseen and the seen, and He will apprise you of what you used to do."

9:95 They will swear by Allah to you, when you return to them, that you may leave them alone. So leave them alone; they are an abomination and their abode is Hell, as a reward for what they used to do.

9:96 They swear to you that you may be well-pleased with them; but should you be well-pleased with them, Allah will not be well-pleased with the sinful people.

Generalizations about Bedouins:

9:97 The desert Arabs are more steeped in unbelief and hypocrisy and are more likely not to know the bounds of what Allah has revealed to His Messenger. Allah is All-Knowing, Wise.

9:98 And some of the desert Arabs regard what they spend as a fine, and await the turns of fortune to go against you. May the evil turn against them. Allah is All-Hearing, All-Knowing.

9:99 And some of the desert Arabs believe in Allah and the Last Day and regard what they spend [in the way of Allah] as a means to get closer to Allah and to earn the prayers of the Messenger. Indeed, that will bring them closer [to Allah]. He will admit them into His Mercy. Allah is truly All-Forgiving, Merciful.

The Bedouins did not always show Allah and His Messenger the respect they thought they deserved and obviously intimidated the Prophet:

Narrated Jubair bin Mutim:

That while he was with Allah's Apostle who was accompanied by the people on their way back from Hunain, the bedouins started begging things of Allah's Apostle so much so that they forced him to go under a Samura tree where his loose outer garment was snatched away.

On that, Allah's Apostle stood up and said to them, "Return my garment to me. If I had as many camels as these trees, I would have distributed them amongst you; and you will not find me a miser or a liar or a coward."

Bukhari 53.376

Narrated Anas bin Malik:

While I was walking with the Prophet who was wearing a Najrani outer garment with a thick hem, a Bedouin came upon the Prophet and pulled his garment so violently that I could recognize the impress of the hem of the garment on his shoulder, caused by the violence of his pull. Then the bedouin said, "Order for me something from Allah's Fortune which you have."

The Prophet turned to him and smiled, and ordered that a gift be given to him.

Bukhari 53.377

Some of the desert Arabs and some of the people of Medina can expect double the punishment.

9:101 And some of the desert Arabs around you (Muhammad) are hypocrites, and some of the people of Medina persist in hypocrisy. You do not know them, but We know them. We shall punish them twice, then they will be afflicted with a terrible punishment (before and after they are thrown into the Fire).

Some confessed that they had lied to avoid going to Tabuk. Allah hints that He will pardon them if they part with some of their wealth. There may also have been some labour involved, revelation 9:105.

9:102 Others have confessed their sins; they mixed a good deed with a bad one (the good deed is confessing sins and the bad one is that they stayed behind when the Muslims marched against the enemy). Perhaps Allah will pardon them. Allah is truly All-Forgiving, Merciful.

9:103 Take of their wealth voluntary alms to purify and cleanse them therewith; and pray for them, for your prayers are a source of tranquility for them. Allah is All-Hearing, All-Knowing.

9:104 Do they not know that Allah is He who accepts the repentance from His servants, and accepts voluntary alms, and that Allah is All-Forgiving, Merciful?

9:105 And say: "Work, for Allah shall see your work, and His Messenger and the believers too. And you shall be brought back (on the Day of Resurrection) to Him Who knows the unseen and the seen, and He will apprise you of what you used to do."

As to any others who, for one reason another avoided the Tabuk trek, Allah will deal with them on Judgement Day.

9:106 And others are deferred to Allah's Decree; He will either punish them or pardon them. And Allah is All-Knowing, Wise.

The Jinn - Introduction

Excerpt from:
Getting to Know Allah, Boreal Books

Of all the inhabitants of the Koran, jinns (Allah refers to them collectively as *the jinn*) are the most fascinating. They are Allah's most versatile and mischievous creation. They even have a chapter of the Koran named after them, surah 72, *The Jinn*. Jinns may not be unlike humans in appearance.

> 7:179 And We have created for Hell multitudes of jinn and men. They have hearts, but do not understand; and they have eyes, but do not see; and they have ears, but do not hear. Those are like cattle, or rather are even more misguided. Those are the heedless ones.

Like the angels, men and the jinn were created to worship Allah, not to look after Him, He can feed himself, and He will feed the wrongdoers, just don't rush Him.

> 51:56 I have not created the jinn and mankind except to worship Me.

> 51:57 I do not desire provision from them and I do not want them to feed Me.

> 51:58 Surely, Allah is the All-Provider, the Mighty One, the Strong.

> 51:59 The wrongdoers will have a portion like the portions of their fellows; so let them not rush Me.

> 51:60 Woe unto the unbelievers on that Day which they have been promised.

Allah created the jinn out of fire before he created man who, in one version of Adam's creation, He moulded out of clay and slime.

> 15:26 And We have created man from potter's clay, moulded out of slime.

> 15:27 And the jinn We created before that from blazing fire.

> ----

> 55:15 And He created the jinn from tongues of fire.

Some people, at one point in time, worshipped the jinn instead of Allah. Allah was under the impression that these wrongly-guided individuals had worshipped His angels. On Judgement Day His angels will set Him straight.

> 34:40 On the Day that He will muster them, then say to the angels: "Are those the ones who used to worship you?"

> 34:41 They will say: "Glory be to You; You are our protector, apart from them." No, rather, they used to worship the jinn, most of them believing in them.

> 34:42 Today, none of them has the power to profit or harm the other, and We will say to the wrongdoer: "Taste the punishment of the Fire which you used to question."

There is no relationship between Allah and the jinn, no matter what they allege, and they will be treated like everybody else on Judgment Day.

> 37:158 And they alleged a kinship between Him and the jinn, whereas the jinn know very well that they will be summoned.

> 37:159 May Allah be exalted above their allegation.

> 37:160 Except for Allah's sincere servants.

> 37:161 Surely, neither you nor what you worship,

> 37:162 Against Him can ever turn anyone;

> 37:163 Except he who will be roasting in Hell.

Allah does not share power with the jinn.

> 6:100 They set up jinn as Allah's partners, although He created them; and they falsely ascribe to Him sons and daughters without any knowledge. Glory be to Him, and highly exalted is He above what they ascribe to Him!

Jinns can be both good and bad.

> 72:11 "And that some of us are righteous and some are less than that for we were of different persuasions;

But even bad jinns can be persuaded to do good if given the proper incentive. Some less than cooperative jinns, with a little prodding from Allah, helped Solomon build the first temple.

> 34:12 And We subjected the wind to Solomon, blowing in the morning the space of a month and in the evening the space of a month; and We smelted for him the fount of brass. Of the jinn some worked before him, by the Leave of

his Lord, and whoever of them swerved from Our Command, We shall make him taste the punishment of the blazing Fire.

34:13 To fashion for him whatever he wished of palaces, statues, basins like water-troughs and immovable cooking-pots. "Work thank-fully, O David's House; for few of My servants are truly thankful."

Some humans sought refuge with the jinn. This Allah may have considered an unnatural relationship considering His use of the word "perversion" in the following verse, where Allah gives the only hint that there may be female jinns.

72:6 "And that some individual humans used to seek refuge with some men of the jinn, and so they increased them in perversion;

The jinn, like the Prophet, once thought that Allah could not raise the dead.

72:7 "And that they thought, as you thought, that Allah will not raise anybody from the dead;

The jinn admit that they have been eavesdropping on Paradise, that Allah is fully aware of what they have been doing, and that even bigger rocks, the comets in the following verse, will now be aimed in their direction if they persist.

72:8 "And that we reached out to heaven, but we found it fill with mighty guards and comets;

72:9 "And that we used to sit around it eavesdropping; but whoever listens now will find a comet in wait for him;

And after listening in on Allah's conversations with his angels, the jinn confess to still not knowing what Allah had in mind for the people on earth.

72:10 "And that we do not know whether ill was intended for whoever is on earth, or whether their Lord intended rectitude for them;

Two verses about the believing jinn's confession-like ramblings from which you can draw your own conclusion.

72:12 "And that we knew that we will not thwart Allah on earth, and that we will not thwart Him by flight;

72:13 "And that when we heard the Guidance, we believed in it; for he who believes in his Lord need not fear to be stinted or over-burdened;

There are the jinn who submit and the jinn who don't.

> 72:14 "And that some us are submitting and some are diverging.' Those who have submitted have surely sought rectitude."

And just like the humans who will not submit, the bad jinn are Hell's firewood. They may have been created "from blazing fire" but that does not mean that they cannot be burnt over and over, especially when no water will be available.

> 72:15 But those who have diverged, have been firewood for Hell;
>
> 72:16 And that had they followed the Right Path, We would have given them abundant water to drink;
>
> 72:17 So as to test them thereby. He who refrains from the mention of His Lord, He will afflict him with terrible punishment.

The jinn may have wanted to intercept the Prophet when he flew up to heaven on al-Burak, taking off from "the farthest Mosque" i.e. Temple Mount in Jerusalem, to meet with Allah.

> 72:18 And that mosques are Allah's; so do not call, besides Allah, upon anyone else;
>
> 72:19 And that when the Servant of Allah (the Prophet Muhammad) got up calling on Him, they almost set upon him in throngs.
>
> 72:20 Say: "I only call upon my Lord, and I do not associate with Him anyone else."
>
> 72:21 Say: "I have no power to harm or guide you rightly."

Not unlike the Christian tradition of an angel rebellion, Allah had a falling out with one of the jinn who would be the progenitor of all evil jinns.

> 18:50 And [remember] when we said to the angels: "Prostrate yourselves to Adam", and they all did except Satan; he was one of the jinn, then he disobeyed the Command of his Lord. Will you, then, take him and his progeny as protectors, besides Me, while they are all your enemies" Evil is the exchange for the wrongdoers!"

Considering the importance of the jinn in the Koran it is surprising that belief in the jinn is not one of the *Pillars of Faith* of Islam.

The Lost Verse

Excerpt from:
Women and the Koran, Boreal Books

If Allah says a public whipping is the punishment for adultery and a wife can avoid even that punishment by calling her husband a liar, why are women accused of adultery still susceptible to being stoned to death in countries where the Koran is the law? Is it because the Prophet was in favour of stoning women, even mothers, for having sexual relations with men other than their husbands?

> Malik related to me from Yaqub ibn Zayd ibn Talha from his father Zayd ibn Talha that Abdullah ibn Abi Mulayka informed him that a woman came to the Messenger of Allah, may Allah bless him and grant him peace, and informed him that she had committed adultery and was pregnant.
>
> The Messenger of Allah, may Allah bless him and grant him peace, said to her, "Go away until you give birth."
>
> When she had given birth, she came to him. The Messenger of Allah, may Allah bless him and grant him peace, said to her, "Go away until you have suckled and weaned the baby."
>
> When she had weaned the baby, she came to him. He said, "Go and entrust the baby to someone."
>
> She entrusted the baby to someone and then came to him. He gave the order and she was stoned.
>
> *Al-Muwatta*

Syed Shahabuddin writing in the Milli Gazette, Indian Muslim's leading English newspaper reminds us that flogging is the punishment for adultery, not stoning and the Koran is the final authority, even the Prophet could not substitute his own opinion. If so, why does Islamic law, in some jurisdictions, give precedence to the example of the Prophet instead of the Koran?

According to Shahabuddin this is because "some [Islamic] scholars support 'Rajm' (stoning) by attributing a statement to the second Caliph Umar (second successor to the Prophet Muhammad) that a revelation on the subject had been received but had been lost."

Narrated Ibn Abbas:

Umar said, "I am afraid that after a long time has passed, people may say, "We do not find the Verses of the Rajam (stoning to death) in the Holy Book," and consequently they may go astray by leaving an obligation that Allah has revealed.

Lo! I confirm that the penalty of Rajam be inflicted on him who commits illegal sexual intercourse, if he is already married and the crime is proved by witnesses or pregnancy or confession."

Sufyan added, "I have memorized this narration in this way."

Umar added, "Surely Allah's Apostle carried out the penalty of Rajam, and so did we after him."

Bukhari 82.816

In a hadith collected by the famous Sunni scholar Ibn Hanbal the verse was eaten by a goat.

[Narrated Aisha] "The verse of the stoning and of suckling an adult ten times were revealed, and they were (written) on a paper and kept under my bed. When the messenger of Allah expired and we were preoccupied with his death, a goat entered and ate away the paper."

So there you have it. When you hear of a woman being stoned or murdered for committing adultery or for having pre-marital relations in conservative Muslim jurisdictions such as Iran, Nigeria or Saudi Arabia the justification just might be this lost verse of the Koran.

Shahabuddin, always helpful, also explains why it is always women who get stoned even though the punishment is supposed to apply equally to both sexes.

"Apart from the brutality of the 'Rajm' (stoning), repugnant to conscience, here is an element of gender injustice in the operation of the traditional law which allows the male partner to get off scot-free, even if he has coerced and raped the female. If the woman lodges a complaint, her complaint is taken as a testimony against herself and, therefore, amounts to admission and requires no further evidence while it is necessary to get 4 witnesses against the man. Also the woman may bear a child, as in Amina's case (Amina Lawal was sentenced to death by stoning by a Nigerian Islamic Sharia Court. Amina had an 8 month old daughter), which is admitted as evidence of zena (guilt) against the woman. Man suffers from no such disability."

~~~~~~~~~~~~~~

Ali, the Prophet's cousin and son-in-law, during the discussions concerning Aisha's suspected adulterous one-night stand (see *The Perfect Wife - A Child Bride's Indiscretion*) told his father-in-law that "Allah has not placed any limits on the choice of a wife. They are plentiful" which would suggest that Ali, who was never a fan of Aisha, favoured that she be stoned.

This has led to speculation that Aisha deliberately got rid of the revelation pertaining to stoning a wife for adultery, after her husband passed away, to avoid being stoned should Ali convinced the Prophet's successor to do what God's Messenger would not do while he was alive.

The Murder of Amr-ben-al Hadra'mi

The First Unbeliever Killed in Allah's Cause

Excerpt from:
Between a Pillar and a Hard Place, Boreal Books

Many of Allah's revelations to His Messenger during his stay in Medina, unlike the revelations the Prophet received during his time in Mecca, have a blood-thirsty, pitiless war-like quality about them. It is during his stay in Medina that the Prophet decides that, if his fellow Arabs will not accept him as Allah's mouthpiece and the Koran as the Word of God on his say-so, he will make them see the light by force.

Minor setbacks, like his initial inability to plunder at will the Meccan caravans passing by Medina, did not deter the Prophet. Unlike his adversaries, God's Messenger had a clear vision of what he wanted to accomplish, and more importantly, the wherewithal to outwit his opponents at almost every turn, combined with a single-minded ruthlessness that knew no bounds. The attack on the twin towers full of innocent men, women and children is a modern manifestation of this innate ruthlessness with which he has imbued many of his followers.

Virgil Gheorghiu, in his admiring biography "Le Prophet Mahomet", from which much of this story finds its inspiration, is not an apologist for the actions of God's Messenger. But, like former nun and author Karen Armstrong who justified the Prophet's dispossession and massacre of the Jews of Medina who saved him and his movement from annihilation, as a "defensive measure", he too condones the attack on what was essentially four farmers taking their goods to market. During the attack, which is made during a holy month when all fighting is forbidden, one farmer is killed.

Gheorghiu repeats the same canard as apologists for the Prophet's questionable actions, in this case, that it was out of necessity that God's Messenger ordered a raid during a sacred month because the believers in Medina were starving to death. Starving in an oasis city famous for its orchards of dates and other fruit bearing trees where the inhabitants more than lived up to the Arab reputation for hospitality stretches credibly to the breaking point.

Is it possible that the cunning farsighted Muhammad planned for the attack to occur when it did so as to do away with, once and for all, the interdiction against warfare during the Sacred Months? An interdiction which he could foresee would play havoc with his plans to Islamisize (sic) the Peninsula by force.

In November 623, having failed to plunder even a single Meccan caravan passing between the Red Sea and Medina, the Prophet changes tactics and decides to attack non-Meccan caravans plying another route. It is all very hush-hush. Even the men who will carry out the first raid don't know what their ultimate target is.

Abdallah-ibn-Jjach, the leader of an eight men raiding party, is given a letter by the Prophet which he is told not to read until he arrives at a famous well, two days ride by camel, west of Medina. The Prophet's instructions tell the group to head in the opposite direction. Two weeks later, they arrive at their destination on the trade route between Mecca and Ta'if where they wait for a caravan making its way from Ta'if to Mecca. Ta'if is a small city about 46 miles or (74 km) south east of Mecca. At an elevation of 6,165 ft. (1,879 m) on the slopes of the Sarawat Mountains the area is conducive to the production of agricultural products such as grapes, roses and honey.

There is still a day left in the sacred month of Rajab when they spot four farmers on their way to Mecca with a cargo of raisins, wine and animal skins. If they wait a day until the end of the sacred month to attack, the small caravan will have reached the precinct of Mecca and will be inviolate. What to do? Follow the Prophet's instructions, which they believe to be from God, or respect god's sacred month. They decide to attack, and one of the four people with the caravan is killed. Amr-ben-al Hadra'mi becomes the first person murdered in Allah's Cause.

When they return to Medina the story of the murder of Hadra'mi during a sacred month has spread far and wide. A scandal has erupted. Believers and unbelievers alike are aghast that anyone would pillage and murder during a sacred month and that this sacrilege would be tolerated. The Prophet's reputation and his holy quest are at stake.

God's Messenger is surprised by the uproar, but is unperturbed. He orders that the puny plunder for which a man was killed (raisins, wine and animal skins) be set aside and not distributed until he has heard from God. A few days later, the Angel Gabriel delivers to the Prophet revelations from Allah that are intended to clarify the rules regarding this killing business during a sacred month.

First, Allah establishes, as a general principle, that killing in retaliation for a killing is allowed during a sacred month; and that killing those who would violate things that are sacred to the believers is justified year round.

2:194 A sacred month for a sacred month; and retaliation

[is allowed] when sacred things [are violated]. Thus whoever commits aggression against you, retaliate against him in the same way. Fear Allah and know that Allah is with those who fear Him.

Next, Allah deals with the question of killing during the sacred months where there is no apparent provocation or reason. In a fine piece of hair splitting, Allah both condemns and condones the murder of Amr-ben-al Hadra'mi. In doing so He implicitly, if not explicitly, gives the believers a licence to kill anyone, anywhere at any time if they honestly believe it will advance the Cause of Allah, such as killing those who would "debar people from Allah's Way", which could be anyone, even other Muslims.

He does not stop there! Believers can also kill anyone at any time, even entire communities, if they fear they will leave Islam, the meaning of "Sedition is worse than murder".

> 2:217 They ask you about the sacred month: "Is there fighting in it?" Say: "Fighting in it is a great sin; but to debar people from Allah's Way and to deny Him and the Sacred Mosque, and to drive its people out of it is a greater sin in Allah's Sight. Sedition is worse than murder." Nor will they cease to fight you until they make you, if they can renounce your religion. Those of you who renounce their religion and die, while they are unbelievers, are those whose works come to grief, [both] in this world and in the Hereafter. And they are the people of the Fire, abiding in it forever.

Today, the sacred months (11 - The Month of Rest; 12 - The Month of Pilgrimage; 1 - The Sacred Month, beginning of the Islamic New Year; and 7 - The Month of Respect) have lost all their pre-Islamic civilizing meaning. Even the holiest of months, *Ramadan*, the ninth month of the Islamic calendar, is not immune to Allah's' fine-spun reasoning when it comes to killing during a period of time considered sacred. Some of the killing done by believers during the last two week of Ramadan (2011):

"29 dead in Iraq mosque suicide bombing" Aug 28

"Attack on UN headquarters [in Abuja by Boko Haram] kills at least 23 people." Aug 26

"Teenage suicide bomber kills 48 at Pakistan mosque" Aug 19

"Roadside bomb kills at least 21 in Afghanistan" Aug 18

"Suicide bombers attack Afghan governor's compound, 22 dead" Aug 14

...

It has been more or less like that since Allah condoned the killing of an innocent man because it was done in His Name.

The Prophet's Last Sermon

Excerpt from:
From Merchant to Messenger, Boreal Books

The second most important document in Islam after the Koran is probably the Prophet's *Farewell Khutba*, his farewell sermon. In his last sermon, delivered on mount Arafat outside Mecca a few months before he died, God's Messenger summarized all the basic beliefs of Islam and all the duties of a Muslim. English translations will usually run less than 1,300 words. Like the Koran, commentators have spoken about the Prophet's last khutba in laudatory terms. If you are not a believer your praise may be more guarded.

The three translations of the Khutba that I consulted all differ in a variety of ways both in content and presentation i.e. the order of what was said. The translation that I have chosen to serve as the template and included in its entirety is the one from S. F. H. Faizi, author of *Sermons of the Prophet*. I would have preferred using Barnaby Rogerson's translation which is rendered in more elegant English but unfortunately his translation is not as complete as Faizi's. Where a segment of Faizi's translation is not as clear as another, I have included the other translator's relevant segment. In one case, I have included what I consider an important declaration on talion law, literally "law as retaliation" whose most common expression is "an eye for an eye", that is in Islamic scholar and author Dr. Muhammad Hamidullah's [1908-2002] translation but not in Faizi's. I have taken on the responsibility of rendering into English quotes from Dr. Hamidullah's French translation of the Khutba. Unless otherwise indicated the translation is from Faizi. Where my understanding of a particular declaration is not clear or where the meaning is self-evident I offer no comment.

The Prophet begins his last khutba with an inspirational panegyric to Allah which reiterates a central concept of Islam that Allah is one indivisible and self-sufficient God, He has "no partner."

> All praise is due to Allah, so we praise Him, and seek His pardon and we turn to Him. We seek refuge with Allah from the evils of ourselves and from the evil consequences of our deeds. Whom Allah guides, there is none to lead him astray; and there is none to guide him aright whom Allah leads astray. I bear witness that there is no God but Allah, the One, having no partner with Him. His is the Sovereignty and to Him is due all praise. He grants life and causes death

and is Powerful over everything. There is no God but Allah, the One; He fulfilled His promise and helped His servant and He alone routed the confederates (tribes allied with the Meccans against the Muslims).

God's Messenger then invites the assembled to listen carefully as this may be the last time they are together to perform the pilgrimage.

O people, listen to my words! for I do not know whether we shall meet again and perform Hajj after this year.

Therefore listen to what I am saying to you very carefully and take these words to those who could not be present here today. (*Rogerson*)

After praising Allah and reminding the faithful that his days are numbered, the Prophet makes what appears to be a universal declaration about all men being equal.

O ye People! Allah says: O people we created you from one male and one female and made you into tribes and nations, so that you are known to one another. Verily in the sight of Allah, the most honoured amongst you is the one who is the most God-fearing. There is no superiority for an Arab over a non-Arab and for a non-Arab over an Arab, nor for the white over the black nor for the black over the white except in piety.

But there is a caveat, "except in piety." All Muslims are equal but Muslims are superior to non-Muslims. This statement also loses some of its lustre when you consider the position of women in Islam and Islam's condoning of slavery. In Islam human rights per se don't exist. In Islam you don't so much have rights as obligations. Most of these obligations are to your God and are spelled out in the Koran or implied in the Prophet's sayings, actions or silent approval of the actions of others done in his presence – his Sunnah. The Koran's emphasis on your obligations to God and the expanse of the Prophet's Sunnah render the Islamic equivalent of universal declaration on human rights largely meaningless if not a contradiction in terms.

After making his less than universal declaration on the brotherhood of men, the Prophet makes a statement about the creation of Adam that, unlike the Koran, is unambiguous: *Adam was created from clay.*

All mankind is the progeny of Adam and Adam was fashioned out of clay.

Following his affirmation about the substance from which the first man was created, the Prophet declares that all debts and undertakings have been remitted or fulfilled, except for one eminently reasonable exception (debts due the House of Allah and supplying of waters to the pilgrimage); that blood feuds from the time of ignorance have been settled or abolished; that the Quraysh, which the Muslim triumph has displaced as the leading tribe of Mecca, not take it so hard.

> Behold! Every claim of privilege whether that of blood or property, is under my feet except that of the custody of Allah's House and supplying of waters to the pilgrimage.

> O people of Quraysh! Do not appear with the burden of the world around your necks, whereas other people may appear [before their Lord] with the rewards of the Hereafter. In that case I shall avail you naught against Allah.

> Behold! All practices of the days of Ignorance are now under my feet. The blood revenges of the days of Ignorance are remitted. And the first claim on blood I abolish is that of Ibne Rabi'ah bin Al-Harith who was nursed in Bani Sa'd and who was killed by the Hudhayls. All interest and usurious dues accruing from the age of Ignorance stand wiped out. And the first amount of interest that I remit is that which Abbas bin Abdul Mutallib had to receive. Verily, it is being remitted entirely.

It was in a cave, on a hill overlooking Mecca that Allah first sent down his revelations confirming the sanctity of a Muslim's life by setting a high price for its taking, and the inviolability of a believer's property by making its taking, without the owners permission, punishable by the amputation of one or both hands. The following declaration is a reminder to the world of the special place that the city of Mecca, the believers, their property, their festivals occupy in Allah's universe.

> O people! Verily your blood, your property and your honour are sacred and inviolable until you appear before your Lord, as the sacred inviolability of this day of yours, this month of yours, and this very town [of yours]. Verily, you will soon meet your Lord and you will be held accountable for your deeds.

> --------

> O my people, just as you regard this day, this city as sacred, so regard the life and property of every Muslim as a sacred trust. Remember that you will indeed meet your Lord, and he will indeed reckon your deeds. *(Rogerson)*

The Prophet on the relationship between husband and wife and how a husband may discipline his wives for acts he deems improper by denying them clothes, food or beating them … but not "too severely."

> O people! Verily, you have got certain rights over your women - and your women have certain rights over you. It is

your right upon them that they must not allow anybody save you to come to your bed and admit none to enter your homes whom you do not like but with your permission. And it is for them not to commit acts of impropriety, which if they do, you are authorized by Allah to separate them from your beds and chastise them, but not severely, and if they refrain, then clothe and feed them properly.

What a wife must not do with her husband's property.

Behold! It is not permissible for a woman to give anything from the wealth of her husband to anyone but with his consent.

All translations consulted on the Prophet's last sermon – to one extent or another – portray women as not having the wherewithal to look after themselves or are not in a position to manage their own affairs. In Dr. Hamidullah's translation women are prisoners in their husband's or father's house. In Faizi's translation, women fair a little better; they are "helpers" provided by Allah to help their male owners manage *their affairs.*

Treat the women kindly, since they are your helpers and are not in a position to manage their affairs themselves. Fear Allah concerning them, for verily you have taken them on the security of Allah and have made their persons lawful unto you by words of Allah.

Treat the women kindly, for verily, they are like prisoners in your house and are incapable of looking after themselves ... (*Hamidullah*)

Women as helpers or prisoners is followed by a reminder of the Koran's strict inheritance rules. In Dr. Hamidullah's translation we find a new rule about a stranger's share of an inheritance which I did not find in the Koran or in the other translations of the Khutba.

O people! Allah, the Mighty and Exalted, has ordained to everyone his due share [of inheritance]. Hence there is no need [of special] testament for a heir [departing from the rules laid down by the Shari'ah].

O people, God has fixed for everyone a rightful share of an inheritance; it is therefore not permitted to make out a will that provides for more than the Lord allows. A stranger's share of an inheritance shall not exceed one third of the total inheritance. (*Hamidullah*)

In the chapter *The Lost Verses,* I refer to an article by Syed Shahabuddin to explain why the stoning of women is still the punishment for adultery in some Islamic jurisdiction when the Koran recommends only a public whipping. According to Shahabuddin, some Islamic jurisdiction still consider stoning to death the appropriated punishment because of a statement attributed to the second Caliph Umar who maintained that a revelation on the subject had been received but had been lost. In some jurisdiction, I suspect, the following admonition from the Prophet may play a role.

> The child belongs to the marriage-bed and the violator of wedlock shall be stoned. And reckoning of their deeds rests with Allah.

Even before the Prophet came along, the Arab patronymic naming nomenclature (a part of a personal name is based on the name of one's father) rested on a father being able to trace his ancestry through his father's name. Therefore, God's Messenger making using your mother's name a serious transgression against God is not entirely out of place.

> He who attributes his ancestry to other than his father or claims his clientship (sic) to other than his master, the curse of Allah is upon him.

The Prophet's warning about spending an eternity in hell, the usual consequence of being cursed by God, for using your mother's name to trace your lineage is followed by a reiteration of the importance of repaying your debts. This would be of concern to a merchant, the occupation of Muhammad before he became God's Messenger, therefore also to be expected.

> All debts must be repaid, all borrowed property must be returned, gifts should be reciprocated and a surety must make good the loss to the assured.

The following declaration only appears in Dr. Hamidullah's translation. Payments in blood and chattel and retaliation in kind are central concepts in Islam, it is only reasonable that the Prophet would remind the faithful of this edict in his last sermon.

> And intentional murder shall be punished according to talion law; where the murderess intention is not clear and the victim is killed using a club or a stone it will cost the perpetrator one hundred camels as blood money. Whoever demands more is a man from the time of ignorance. (Hamidullah)

The only universal declaration in the entire Khutba i.e. no exceptions!

> Beware! No one committing a crime is responsible for it but himself. Neither the child is responsible for the crime of his father, nor the father is responsible for the crime of his child.

The Prophet again reminds the believers that it is a crime to steal from another Muslim.

> Nothing of his brother is lawful for a Muslim except what he himself gives willingly. So do not wrong yourselves.

What God allows no man can deny. In the face of this bleak reality, it is to the Prophet's credit that he asks the faithful to take good care of their slaves.

> And your slaves! see that you feed them with such food as you eat yourselves, and clothe them with the clothes as you yourselves wear.

A plea that Muslims refrain from fighting each other after he is gone, and to return entrusted goods to their rightful owner:

> Beware that you go not astray after me and strike one another's necks. He who [amongst you] has any trust with him, he must return it to its owner.

A declaration on the suitably of black *mangled* slaves as military commanders or rulers – the meaning of Amir:

> If a mangled black slave is appointed your Amir, listen to him, and obey him provided he executes the Ordinance of the Book of Allah amongst you.

Confirming that he is the last of God's messengers and Islam the last religion:

> O people! There is no Prophet to come after me and there would be no Ummah to form after you.
>
> ---------
>
> O my people! No prophet or apostle will come after me and no new faith will be born. (*Rogerson*)

The Prophet on his legacy:

> Verily I have left amongst you that which would never lead you astray, the Book of Allah, and the Sunnah of His Messenger, which if you hold fast, you shall never be misled. And beware of transgressing the limits set in the matters of Deen (the faith of a Muslim; his party cry. *Wiki*), for it is transgression of [the proper bounds of] Deen, that brought destruction to many people before you.
>
> --------
>
> Reason well, therefore my people, and understand my word which I convey to you. I leave behind me two things, the Qur'an and my example, the Sunnah, and if you follow these you will never go astray. (*Rogerson*)

No comment.

> Verily the Satan is disappointed at ever being worshipped in this land of yours, but if obedience in anything [short of worship is expected that is]: he will be pleased in matters you may be disposed to think insignificant, so beware of him in the matters of your Deen.

A reminder of the five mandatory pillars of the Faith (I interpret "worship your Lord" as the first pillar, the Shahadah, the declaration of faith).

> Behold! worship your Lord; offer prayers five times a day; observe fast in the month of Ramadan; pay readily the Zakat (obligatory charity, the third pillar of Islam) on your property; and perform pilgrimage to the House of God and obey your rulers and you will be admitted to the Paradise of your Lord.

No comment.

> O people! Postponement [of a sacred month] is only an excess of disbelief whereby those who disbelieve are misled; they allow it one year and forbid it [another year] that they may make up the number of the months which Allah hath hallowed, so that they allow that which Allah hath forbidden. And verily the time hath adopted the shape of the day when Allah hath created the heavens and the earth. And Lo! The number of months with Allah is twelve months. Four of them are sacred. Three are consecutive months and the Rajab, in between the months of Jumadius sani and Sha'aban.

Spread the word.

> Let him that is present, convey it unto him who is absent. For many people to whom the message is conveyed may be more mindful of it than the audience.
>
> --------
>
> All those who listen to me shall pass on my words to others and those to others again; and may understand my words better than those who listen to me directly. *(Rogerson)*

In Faizi's translation the Prophet ends his khutba by asking his audience "And if you were asked about me, what would you say?" With one voice, it is said, the thousands who had listened to the Prophet shouted "We bear witness that you have conveyed the trust and discharged your ministry and looked to our welfare." After which, again according to Faizi, the Prophet lifted his forefinger towards the sky and then pointing towards the people said "O Lord: Bear Thou witness unto it" three times.

In Dr. Muhammad Hamidullah's translation the Prophet ends his address to the faithful with "peace be with you" and this is also how I would like to end our discussion - *peace be with you.*

The Satanic Verses

Excerpt from:
Women and the Koran, Boreal Books

Pre-Islamic Arabs worshipped three goddesses, al-Lat, al-Uzza, and Manat who they believed to be the daughters of the moon god "al-Ilah" (Allah). Pre-Islamic Arabs had no problems with a spiritual existence that included gods and goddesses. The Prophet's tribe, the Quraysh, used to chant, as they circumambulated the Ka'ba, "Al-Lat, and al-Uzza and Manat, the third, the other; indeed these are exalted gharaniq (cranes); let us hope for their intercession." (*F. E. Peters, The Hajj, p 3-41*)

The Meccans, when the Prophet showed up with his army, gave up without a fight after God's Messenger assured them that Allah, in two revelations, had informed him that He had no objections to the Meccans continuing to worship al-Lat, al-Uzza, and Manat after they became Muslims. These revelations are what are known as the *Satanic Verses.*

> These are the exalted cranes (al-Lat, al-Uzza, and Manat)
>
> Whose intercession [with Allah] is to be hoped for.

The next day, after he had complete control of their city, the Prophet told the Meccans that it was all the devil's doing; that Satan had intruded on his conversations with Allah the previous night, and in the morning Allah had set him straight and al-Lat, al-Uzza, and Manat were history and the verses the Prophet had received the previous night were stricken from the Koran.

> 22:52 We have not sent a Messenger or Prophet before you but when he recited the Devil would intrude into his recitation. Yet Allah annuls what the Devil had cast. Then Allah establishes His Revelations. Allah is All-Knowing and Wise.

How could the Devil do that? Because Allah let him, for His usual somewhat convoluted reasons!

> 22:53: So as to make what Satan casts a temptation to those in whose hearts there is a sickness, and to those whose hearts are hard. The wrongdoers are indeed in profound discord!

22:54 And so that those who have been given the knowledge might understand that it is the truth from your Lord and so believe in it. Then their hearts will submit to it. Allah will certainly guide the believers to a straight path.

Even if it was His doing i.e. He allowed the devil to intrude on His conversations, Allah is incensed that anyone would associate Him with females whether they be goddesses daughters, even angels.

53:19 Have you, then, seen al-Lat and al-'Uzza?

53:20 And Manat, the third one, the other?

53:21 Do you have the male and He has the female?

53:22 That indeed is an unjust division.

53:23 These are mere names you (*Meccan unbelievers*) and your fathers have named, for which Allah did not send down any authority. They only follow conjecture and what the souls desire; yet Guidance (*the Qur'an*) has come to them from their Lord.

53:24 Or will man have whatever he wishes?

16:57 And they ascribe to Allah daughters [glory be to Him!], but to themselves what they desire (sons).

16:58 And if the birth of a daughter is announced to any of them, his face turns black, and he is enraged.

16:59 He hides from the people on account of the evil news broken to him; should he keep it in humiliation or bury it in the ground? Evil is what they judge!

16:60 As for those who do not believe in the Hereafter, theirs is the evil exemplar; but Allah's is the sublime exemplar. He is the Almighty, the Wise.

16:61 Were Allah to take mankind to task for their wrongdoing, He would not leave upon it (the earth) a single creature; but He reprieves them until an appointed term. Then, when their term comes, they will not delay nor advance it a single hour.

16:62 And they ascribe to Allah what they themselves dislike (daughters). Their tongues utter the lie that theirs will be the best reward. There is no doubt that the Fire awaits them, and that they will be left [there].

Verse 17:40, which follows, is doubly confusing since angels *have no gender,* although they do take the male form, minus the genitalia, to facilitate communications with humans.

> 17:40 Has your Lord, then, favoured you with sons and taken to Himself females from among the angels? Surely, you are uttering a monstrous thing.

If you do not believe in the Hereafter you are an unbeliever; and only an unbeliever would give angels female names (give them a gender, and a female one at that), revelation 53:27, knowing Allah's low opinion of the fair sex and His high regard for His angels.

> 53:25 For to Allah belongs the last and the first life.

> 53:26 How many an angel is there in heavens whose intercession avails nothing, except after Allah gives leave to whoever He wishes and is well-pleased with.

> 53:27 Those who do not believe in the Hereafter will surely give the angels the names of females.

> 53:28 Yet, they have no knowledge thereof. They only follow conjecture, but conjecture avails nothing regarding truth.

> 53:29 So turn away from him who has given up Our Reminder (*the Qur'an*) and only desire the present life.

> 53:30 That is their attainment in knowledge. Your Lord indeed knows better than those who have strayed from His Path, and He knows better those who are well-guided.

For one brief shining moment, because of the alleged intervention by Satan, Allah had female partners. Just imagine what Islam would have been like if Allah had acknowledged needing the company of females, whether they be goddesses or mortals. With females for company would Allah have been such a vengeful god, so easily irritated, so quick to kill and terrorize? I don't think so.

Had Allah acknowledged that daughters were just as valuable as sons instead of being insulted that some would attribute themselves sons and to Him females, would women in many countries where the Koran is the law be so harshly treated. Probably not. The denial of the existence of al-Lat, al-Uzza, and Manat marked the end of the Arab civilization of which historian Robert Montagne wrote (my translation) "I am not aware in the entire history of civilisation of a more gracious, more loving, more vibrant society than that of the Arabs before Islam."

Index of Abrogated Verses

24:3, 28	24:4, 29	24:6, 45	24:27, 28
24:31, 30	24:54, 67	24:58, 31	25:63, 67
25:68, 55	25:69, 55	26:224, 56	26:225, 56
26:226, 56	27:92, 67	28:55, 67	29:46, 74
29:50, 67	30:60, 67	31:23, 67	32:30, 68
33:48, 68	33:52, 32	34:25, 68	35:23, 68
36:76, 68	37:174, 68	37:175, 68	37:178, 68
38:70, 68	38:88, 68	39:3, 68	39:13, 33
39:14, 68	39:15, 68	39:36, 68	39:39, 68
39:40, 68	39:41, 68	39:46, 68	40:12, 69
40:55, 69	40:77, 69	41:34, 69	42:5, 33
42:6, 69	42:15, 69	42:20, 53	42:23, 34
42:39, 57	42:41, 57	42:48, 69	43:83, 69
43:89, 69	44:59, 69	45:14, 69	46:9, 47
46:35, 69	47:4, 69	50:39, 70	50:45, 70
51:19, 50	52:31, 70	52:45, 70	52:48, 70
53:29, 70	53:39, 34	54:6, 70	58:12, 35
60:8, 36	60:11, 70	68:44, 70	68:48, 70
70:5, 70	70:42, 70	73:1, 36	73:5, 36
73:10, 70	73:11, 70	73:19, 36	74:11, 70
75:16, 37	76:8, 70	76:24, 70	76:29, 70
80:12, 36	81:28, 37	86:17, 71	88:21, 71
88:22, 71	88:23, 71	95:8, 71	109:6, 71